In happy and loving memory of my sister Jean,
with whom I travelled so far and saw so much.

Jean Argles Née Owtram
November 7th 1925-April 2nd 2023

9th June 1929. picnic we had on Flarshaw. Jill, our Nannie, Jean, Pat, Aunty Doll, Pat, Walter, Cary, Paul & Christopher.

Mrs. Kirk & me in my nursery. I am one day old. That is my cot behind me, it is covered in little pink frills, and has bunches of roses & forget-me-nots here & there.

Grannie & me. I am three days old.

Tuesday 9th Aug. Mrs. Kirk, my bear, Cassie. Gerry gave it to me when she came to tea.

Friday 3rd Aug. Grandpa & Grannie and Mummy - Nanny & I motored to Preston in Dad's.

Grandpa, Grannie & me.

Volume V

Beach

JUNE
30 Days
Summer Solstice, Longest Day

7th Feb. 1929. When Windermere froze. Uncle Sidney, Jean, Pat and

who asks tv producer Pat
what kind of a Christmas
needs plenty of time to
answer.

...ent Christmas Day making a
...lephone calls and at 4.45 on
...

flask of black coffee to Television Centre.
She was en route to produce an
emergency appeal for the Nicaraguan
earthquake.
Dozens of BBC staff were involved in
complex arrangements to get the appeal
on BBC 1 at 10.45 pm on 27 December.

Denis Mann of Secretariat rang Pat in
Lancaster where she had gone for
Christmas with her husband Ray Davies
of The World Tonight and her daughter
Ruth, a secretary in Registry. He told her
that a request for an appeal had been
relayed by Lord Hill and it was likely to
be scheduled by Paul Fox for Wednesday
... someone who knew
... the appeal. Her
...

Recalling N-W space explore...

...st to discover the Transit
... Venus.
...on was the first feature
... "space geometry." By
...ching the black mass of
... cross the face of the
...using observational justify
...st of the earth's interna-
...scientists were able to
... the distance of the...
...from the sun.

...phenomenon is
...natural, and is
...eas about science
...the crest of the
...over the past few
...ably he has
... from the use of
...take to make the
... discoveries he...
... that was in 1769,
...

STR... EY PRIVATE ...

Mrs ...gham...
St ...
...

Three days old Grandieann in the ...

15 p.m. All clear just gone c...
...am, during which I had a...
...t of her window, + π put...
slacks, got the warning (red) +...
...2 alarms which Daddy was...

...they...
...each...
...ms to...
...are no...
Buck...
...spitals +...
...nost st....
...Spices, of...
...to flit...
...the D.S.C...
action...
...for which h...
...

Pat Jean + their animals
probably taken in the spring of
Pat's beloved Koko is sitting o...
...ways head.

Margaret Dale, Pat tracked Dame Mar...
to a London hotel and left a message.
The rest of the family were ...
Christmas lunch," said Pat. "I sat in ...
father's unheated sunroom where ...
keeps the phone." Dame Margot ...
from London that night and agreed ...
the appeal.
On Boxing morning Pat, her hu...
and daughter who also offered to ...
were up at 4 am to drive to Londo...
10.30 they met Denis Mann at his ...
had made over 40 calls from his ...
Kingston to keep the necessar...
departments informed. Dame ...
missing her regular ballet practice...
worked on the script until lun...
News VT compiled ... shot...
Nicaragua. Newsroom provided...
tapes, Library supplied inf...
emergency graphics were ...
presentation staff on duty ...
Hubbard, Nick Franks, John F...
and Bruce Goddard — were ...
...

MIRROR BOOKS

1

Published in Great Britain and Ireland in 2023 by
Mirror Books, a Reach PLC business.

www.mirrorbooks.co.uk
@TheMirrorBooks

Print ISBN 9781915306340
eBook ISBN 9781915306357

Cover and Design by Rick Cooke
Edited by Christine Costello

Printed and bound in Great Britain by
CPI Group (UK) Ltd, Croydon, CR0 4YY

CENTURY SISTERS
Our Hundred Years

Patricia and Jean Owtram

with Chris Manby

MIRROR BOOKS

As one gets closer to one's centenary year, of course one can't help but look back. What a lot of change we have seen in our two lifetimes.

This is our second book. In the first, 'Codebreaking Sisters: Our Secret War', we wrote about our years in the women's services during World War Two. It's a part of our lives that we've talked about often – at schools and at history festivals, on podcasts and on television. However, our time in uniform, exciting and important though it was, lasted but a handful of years. We have lived through many other epoch-defining events before and since, including the Great Depression, the Moon Landings and the dreadful Covid 19 pandemic.

When we were born, most women in the United Kingdom were still denied the vote. It wasn't until 1928 that the Representation of the People Act brought Universal Suffrage to the United Kingdom. Since then, we've seen more prime ministers than we can count. Our grandmothers would have been astonished by the fact that three of those prime ministers have been women.

We have lived during the reigns of four kings and a beloved queen. Like Queen Elizabeth II, who was our contemporary, we enjoyed a very happy childhood in the '20s and '30s. We are often asked to revisit that childhood in our talks, particularly since Downton Abbey has brought the inter-war years to our television screens.

We're fortunate to have come from a family of letter writers and doubly fortunate that our mother Dorothy Owtram had the foresight to keep many of the letters that came her way. Together with a newly-discovered cache of childhood diaries, notes and essays, those letters have helped to jog our memories and enabled us to better piece together a picture of our early years in a world that seems at first glance to be very different from the one we live in now. Yet, digging a little deeper, so much remains the same.

While on the surface our childhood was one of parties and ponies, pageants and 'pretends' that might have come straight from a Nancy Mitford novel, the '20s and '30s were a time of great social upheaval. We were born into a world still suffering the aftershocks of the Great War and the Spanish Flu pandemic that followed hot on its heels, killing 50 million people world-wide. A 1938 letter to our mother from her naval officer brother 'Uncle Tid' reveals geo-political concerns that have striking echoes in the news headlines of today. When it comes to war and plague, there's little comfort in the feeling that we've 'seen it all before'.

But there is something eternal about the happy times too. Our childhood games and teenage passions were not so different from those of 21st century children, as the lists of 'heroes' we scribbled into the backs of our diaries show. Even our sibling squabbles will be familiar to any modern parent.

We're also including here some diary extracts and letters

from the early years of the war, before we joined up, both signed the Official Secrets Act, and were forbidden from keeping diaries or writing to each other about our work. There are anecdotes and letters from our post-war lives too, which show how the war enabled us to break away from the usual expectations for women of our era and class, to forge two interesting careers in fields our grandmothers hadn't even heard of.

One doesn't expect to live for a whole century. It's astonishing. It seems to have happened so quickly. In some ways, it seems a little 'over the top' to have been around for so long, like the famous giant tortoise on Saint Helena. But how glad we are to have got here and to be here together, looking back at all the good things that have come our way and still enjoying the very special sisterly bond that began more than nine and a half decades ago. And what a privilege it is to be able to share our stories, and those of some of the people we have known and loved, with you.

Patricia Davies and Jean Argles

PART ONE

Before the War

CHAPTER ONE

Pat

We grew up at Newland Hall in Dolphinholme, a village which lies under the westward shoulders of the Pennines, the hills that run like a spine up the middle of the North of England, dividing our county of Lancashire from next-door Yorkshire. In August the hills are covered with the soft grape-coloured bloom of heather. Lower down, the countryside is very green and fresh and cool, with a climate tempered by the Gulf Stream flowing just off its coast. Among the woods and fields stand small square farmhouses, built, like their barns and pig-styes, of the grey local stone, sometimes whitewashed, with blue-slate roofs. The farms have curious names like Starbank, Croft Height, Hare Appletree and Isle of Skye.

Dolphinholme is not old as English villages go, although people have lived for centuries near the curve of the River Wyre in Dolphinholme Bottom. There are traces of early occupation all around. There was a 'henge', ten miles south at Bleasdale. Not nearly so big as Stonehenge, and made of wood, but a significant prehistoric monument all the same. The straight paved Roman road leading to the fort at Carlisle and the westward end of the Hadrian's Wall passed nearby. All that can be seen of that road now is where it crossed the river, just below the village. The Roman bridge was of fine squared stones, and its supporting wall still stands against the riverbank, just as they built it, though the bridge itself vanished long ago. You can also see the raised causeway that ran up to the bridge under the grass of a field, and no doubt from the air the whole line of the ancient highway might be traced, running straight as an arrow flight across the fields towards Lancaster on the river Lune, which the Romans called Lunae Castrum, the Fort of the Moon.

Lancaster Museum is full of Roman coins, arms and pottery found in the district. Our great local figure, however, was John O'Gaunt, military leader and statesman, fourth son of Edward III and father of Henry IV, whose frowning castle on the hill dominates the countryside. In such veneration was John O'Gaunt held, when, as he was riding through the town one day, his horse lost a shoe, his loyal citizens preserved that shoe where it fell. There you will see it – not perhaps the original, which wore out and has been replaced a number of times, but still, a horseshoe – embedded in the middle of the pavement at the junction of Penny Street, Market Street and Cheapside.

Our district was wild country until well after the middle ages. There must have been some Viking settlement, of which traces survive in names – for instance, the Pennines are known to everyone as 'the fells'; though on the whole the local vocabulary is good Anglo-Saxon – a cowshed is a 'shippen', an ignorant man 'knows nowt about owt' and 'upper' and 'lower' in place names are 'over' and 'nether'.

In the seventeenth and eighteenth centuries the countryside was gradually reclaimed from moorland, and one by one the small, neat farmhouses were built – each house built straight onto the end of its barn, with a stone panel over the door giving the date in long-tailed figures. Though some of the houses are older, including the beautiful old water-mill by the Wyre with its whitewashed walls several feet thick, almost all of Dolphinholme village was built early in the nineteenth century to house workers at the new textile mill in the valley.

Dolphinholme perhaps really dates from 1784 when a spinning mill for cotton, and later worsted, was set up, worked by water-power from the Wyre. It was probably the first mill ever to be lighted by gas produced on the premises. In its heyday the mill worked a 24-hour shift, and tradition has it that the workers shared the cottages in Dolphinholme Bottom, one lot falling into the beds the others had just vacated. The mill didn't last a century, finally closing in 1869, unable to compete with those nearer the railways and the canal, where coal was cheaper.

During our childhood, the stump of Dolphinholme mill chimney was still visible at the end of the village. It loomed behind St Peter and St Mark in the village church's stained-glass window. Standing at the top of the village the church itself is deceptive. It was built by Austin and Paley of Lancaster, and dates from 1899 but looks very much older. The view across the river from the churchyard up to the hills, with only the sounds of running water, wind and birds, must be one of the most restful in the world. Inside, the church's great charm is its simplicity. The east window is of clear glass, with a moving pattern beyond it of branches and leaves from the tall trees in the churchyard – an endless diversion and pleasure from our old family pew.

To be truthful, the village of Dolphinholme as we knew it as children was not beautiful. The steep wooded valley, the brown river, the line of fells behind, the fertile farming country around it – those were beautiful. But the cottages themselves, built as cheaply as possible in bleak grey rows, in some cases built so badly that the walls cracked and they had to be pulled down, were unfortunately rather ugly. Nor were they too convenient – in the 1920s and '30s, half the houses in the villages still had no water (the more fortunate half had one cold tap to each cottage), and every housewife had to fetch what she needed from the faucet at the end of the village street in a bucket, or send her children along for it.

Grand as it may sound, our family home, Newland Hall was originally a little four-square 18th century farmhouse like the others, built of sandstone from a local quarry. Its name derived from that reclamation of farming land from the moors. Our great-grandfather Henry Owtram built extra rooms onto the original farmhouse and, against the advice of his architect, moved into it while the rooms were still damp, hoping the local gravel soil would benefit his poor health. He died within a year, and though his widow managed to plan and establish the garden very well, she and her children had to move out to live with relations in the south.

Henry Owtram's eldest son, Herbert Hawkesworth was whisked away from school to go into the family cotton spinning business so he could support his widowed mother.

He did well, married and moved his growing family back to Newland Hall. He added more improvements including a front porch and a billiard room.

Herbert Hawkesworth Owtram was our grandfather, known to us as Grandboffin. He married Ethel and they had four children – all sons. Their second son, Henry Cary Owtram, known as Cary, was our father.

CHAPTER TWO

Jean

Our father Cary came of age during The Great War and, as soon as he was able, joined the Royal Marines for the last of the fighting. When the war ended, he returned to Lancashire and set about making plans for the future. But fate called Cary back to his childhood home when, shortly before he was to be married, his mother – our grandmother – Ethel Owtram died.

Ethel, called Effie by her loved ones, was born and raised in Lytham St Annes. She was known by all who met her as a vivacious and elegant woman, who loved to throw parties and would find any excuse to host a dance. On the occasion of Effie's marriage to our grandfather, a composer friend wrote a lively gavotte in her honour. We still have a collection of the dance cards Effie had printed for the parties she hosted and a specially-made shepherdess costume that Effie wore for a fancy dress ball.

As the new mistress of Newland Hall, Effie quickly made a great impression on the local community with her generous and open-hearted nature. When the Great War began and her eldest son, our Uncle Tom, left to fight in France with the King's Own Royal Lancaster Regiment, Effie set to work, setting up a Prisoners of War Care

Committee to support those King's Own soldiers taken captive overseas.

Effie organised a well-attended concert at the Shireshead Institute, which raised plenty of money to send parcels of socks and other necessities to the POWs. A collection of the letters Effie received from those soldiers is now held at The King's Own Royal Regiment Museum in Lancaster. The letters reveal how very welcome Effie's efforts were, particularly to those soldiers languishing in field hospitals waiting anxiously for news from home; soldiers like Private Nicholas Goulding, whose sister Matilda, a nun, wrote to Effie, 'He cannot find words to express the gratitude he owes you and I must confess I too am at a loss to express my admiration and sincere gratitude at your constant generosity… I have often asked our Divine Lord to inspire some kind friend to do this act of mercy for me and you are the kind friend, dear Madame.'

With her eldest son fighting in France, Effie also knew something of the anxiety of those left at home waiting for news from the front. Uncle Tom came home safely at the end of the war but poignantly, over 20 years later, Effie's second son, our father, would find himself a Japanese POW in Singapore. Alas, our father would not benefit from the kindness of people like our grandmother, because the Japanese did not pass on gifts from home or even Red Cross parcels to the prisoners in their camps.

There were lighter occasions for Effie to exercise her empathy too. Our mother told us how, after Effie died, a local woman – let's call her Mrs Smith – regaled her with a story that perfectly illustrates Effie's kindness and civilising influence. Mrs Smith described how her husband, a good man at heart, had developed a worrying habit of getting so drunk from an evening at The Fleece Inn, our nearest pub, that he would often fail to make it all the way home. Giving up at about halfway, he would curl up in a ditch like an animal and try to sleep off his drunkenness there.

'What can I do about it, Mrs Owtram?' Mrs Smith had asked Effie in desperation.

'I'll have a word with him,' Effie promised.

And that's exactly what she did. When she next saw him, Effie said to the woman's wayward husband, 'I'd like to make a bargain with you, Mr Smith. If you promise never again to go to sleep in a ditch on your way home from The Fleece, then I promise I shall never go to sleep in a ditch either.'

Effie's humorous approach to the problem worked. From that moment on, bound by his promise to our grandmother, Mr Smith always made it home from the pub. Hearing stories such as this made us very sorry not to have known Effie except through such second-hand tales.

Effie's lightness belied a private struggle with depression but her sudden death at the age of 51, came as a shock to everyone. It was a devastating blow for her family at Newland Hall.

Effie's two younger sons – our uncles Godfrey and Bill – were away at school when their mother died. Naturally Grandboffin wanted to be the one to break the news, so, when the time came for Godfrey and Bill to come home, he instructed the friend who went to fetch them by train not to mention anything about the tragedy that had unfolded in their absence. What Grandboffin and his friend didn't know was that our young uncles had already read the terrible news in the local papers and all that sad journey home, they thought they were protecting the friend sent to fetch them by not talking about their mother's death. How difficult it must have been for them both, still quite young children, to suppress their personal pain out of misplaced respect for the feelings of others.

Grandboffin did his best to help his children through their grief but he was a man of his age, a true Victorian, and he was not about to try to raise two motherless boys on his own. Deciding that his youngest sons needed a woman about the house, six months after Effie died he asked our father and mother, who had only recently married, to move in so that Mummy could be a steadying, maternal influence on her young brothers-in-law.

It must have been a difficult proposition— the newly-weds doubtless had many plans of their own – but they dutifully moved into Newland Hall to give Bill and Godfrey a valuable sense of stability in their time of grieving. Little did they know that the move back to our father's childhood home would be permanent.

Our mother, Dorothy Daniel, was a Preston girl. Her father had been adjutant of the King's Own Depot in Lancashire before he moved to the Record Office at Preston's Fulwood

Barracks. Lieut. Col. Daniel, whom we all knew as our grand-father 'Pops', was a Yorkshireman through and through. However our grandmother Agnes Daniel, a Saumaurez by birth, was from the Channel Island of Guernsey. Thus our mother's childhood was heavily influenced by French culture too.

Dorothy was known to her family and friends by her nickname, Bunty. Educated by governesses until her mid-teens, she spent only a brief period at boarding school, before leaving to join the Women's Land Army in 1917. She threw herself into the war effort, working on a large farm just outside Preston. One of Bunty's duties was to drive a truck loaded with fruit and vegetables to the local market. As one of the first women in Preston to have a driving licence, she must have turned heads as she drove through the town.

Bunty Daniel certainly turned Cary Owtram's head. Our father was entranced by the fiercely independent and confident young woman he saw behind the wheel of the farm truck. Shortly after they met, Bunty came into a small inheri-tance upon turning 21 and immediately bought herself a car. With transport of her own, she could easily drive to meet Cary at the half-way point between their homes, which were 15 miles apart. Between those meetings, Cary and Bunty would write flirtatious letters to one another, pretending that it was not them but their cars that were falling in love. Later, they gave each other nicknames. Cary was 'Moulu' and Bunty was 'Moulette'.

After a short courtship, Cary and Bunty were married at Christ Church Fulwood, just north of Preston. The marriage, in August 1921, was reported in the local papers. It was celebrated by the Archdeacon of Lancaster in front of a large congregation. The church was decorated with rambler roses and our mother, who was attended by four bridesmaids, wore a dress of white and silver brocade, with sleeves and side-panels of georgette ivory. Her train was made of old Brussels lace, while her veil was held in place by a wreath of orange blossom. She carried a bouquet of pale pink roses and lily of the valley. After the ceremony, 200 guests were invited to a reception at the Park Hotel, then Preston's most prestigious hotel.

Later that day our parents left for a honeymoon in the Scottish Highlands – a part of the United Kingdom that would come to hold a special place in all our hearts. They travelled in a car given to them by Grandboffin. As the local paper reported, our mother's going away outfit was almost as glamorous as her wedding gown. She wore a dress in lavender blue georgette, with a large silver hat and white fur coat.

After the honeymoon, our parents returned to their first home in Preston for a few short weeks before Grandboffin persuaded them to live with him at Newland Hall. Our father had already found Bunty to be a true and supportive partner in his grief and – as Grandboffin had hoped – she enveloped her young brothers-in-law with love.

Two years later, Bunty and Cary began their own family and that is where our story of sisterhood begins.

CHAPTER THREE

Pat

We have our mother to thank for much of the early content of this book. Bunty was, as we've mentioned, a great letter writer and someone who carefully held on to the letters she in turn received from friends and family all over the world. She also kept a diary, and, when I was born in the summer of 1923, began a 'baby book' to document my early years.

The book's dark brown leather cover is tattered and well-worn by now, but the pages inside are still pristine, despite the many times Jean and I have taken the book out to marvel at its contents. The pictures and stories in the baby book provide a lovely record of my babyhood and, later, Jean's too. The early entries are edged with our mother's delicate pen and ink drawings; she drew frames made of curling vines and dainty flowers and tiny yellow ducklings. Our mother was a talented artist and she especially loved to draw cartoons. During the Great War, when she wasn't driving a truck or digging up vegetables, she illustrated the Women's Land Army magazine, 'The Landswoman' with her clever sketches.

The black and white photographs pasted to each page of the baby book offer a glimpse into an England with one foot still in the Victorian age. As was common at the time in families of our social class, our parents employed a nanny to help ease them into parenthood. My first nanny was one Mrs Ledger – 'Nanny Kent', as we children would come to know her. Nanny Kent had a reputation as someone who knew how to 'bring on' sickly babies. She was a rather large lady, with a deep voice and an enormous bosom that offered great comfort to the children she looked after. I adored her. According to the baby book, I gave my very first smile to Nanny Kent during a heatwave in the summer of 1923 when I was a few weeks old. I blew her my first kiss later that same year, during my first proper holiday to Scotland.

The baby book contains many photographs of that summer, during which we went to the seaside at Morecambe to escape the worst of the heat. I'm pictured sitting on Nanny Kent's lap in front of a row of old-fashioned bathing machines – small square shed-like contraptions on wheels, in which people could be conveyed straight into the sea so that no-one might see them in their swimming costumes before they were modestly up to their necks in the water. Despite the heatwave, in every picture taken that summer Nanny Kent is wearing a heavy black coat and a hat, and looks thoroughly Edwardian, like the Grandma in the famous Giles cartoons. As far as Nanny Kent was concerned, the weather was no excuse for being under-dressed.

Nanny Kent's domain was the nursery. The nursery at Newland Hall was on the first floor of the house in what had once been my paternal grandparents' bedroom. It was a beautiful, large, light room with a big bay window that looked out onto the lawn sweeping down to the pond, but, understandably, Grandboffin had decided to sleep elsewhere after our grandmother's death.

One afternoon, shortly after I was born, Nanny Kent and I were in the nursery together – she sitting in her usual chair, watching over me as I slept in my crib – when an elegant woman, dressed in old-fashioned clothes, came into the room. The woman made her way towards me, and stood by the side of the crib to gaze down upon me with a soft smile upon her face. After a moment or so, she turned to Nanny Kent, nodded a polite goodbye, then made her way noiselessly back out into the corridor. Her long skirt made no sound as it swished across the carpet and she said not a single word.

When my mother came in to see me a short while later, Nanny Kent asked, 'Who was that lady who came up to see Baby Pat this afternoon?'

'What lady?' asked my mother, who had been entertaining friends to tea in the drawing room. 'Nobody has been upstairs today but me so far as I know.'

The following day, Nanny Kent drew my mother's attention to an old family photograph on the nursery mantelpiece.

'There she is,' she said. 'That was the lady I saw.'

I can only imagine my mother's surprise when she realised that Nanny Kent was pointing to an image of her late mother-in-law, in one of the few photographs of Effie that Grandboffin hadn't had put away. The memory of Effie was very painful to my grandfather. Though I had been christened Ethel Patricia in her honour, I had quickly become Pat because he didn't even like to hear his late wife's name.

My mother and Nanny Kent resolved not to tell Grand-boffin about the ghostly visitation. As far as we know, that was the only time anyone ever saw a ghost at Newland Hall but I like to think that our grandmother might have looked in on Jean and our brother Bob when they were babies too.

I was a rather grumpy little girl at times. I was told that one Sunday morning I cried so loudly in church that the vicar offered up a special prayer for 'the wailing babe'. In the baby book, my mother writes about an occasion when her car broke down, with me in my carry cot in the back. As we wait-ed by the side of the road, a fellow motorist, who was driv-ing an expensive Rolls Royce, stopped to offer us a lift. His kindness went unrewarded. Once inside the beautiful car, I started bawling and would not stop until we reached our destination. The gallant driver must have wondered what he had let himself in for, joking with my mother that there was 'no need for a horn today'.

Though it was still unusual at the time, the women in our family were all keen drivers. Our mother remained enthu-siastic about driving throughout her life, always keeping up with the latest developments in motoring. She was very practical. I remember being in the car with her one afternoon – still a small child at the time – when the engine suddenly caught fire. Our mother quickly pulled over and, with nothing else to hand, put out the flames with handfuls of gravel from the road. The gravel worked very well as a fire extinguisher but did nothing for the health of the engine.

One of our mother's favourite cars was a white Hillman Minx, bought in the early thirties. She loved its economy and efficiency. It was in that car that she taught my Uncle Bill to drive (Bill still came home to Newland Hall in the school holidays and was like a big brother to us). I remember sitting in the back, listening to them bickering as we drove around the country lanes.

'Yes, Bunty. I can see that car coming towards us!' Bill shouted in exasperation.

When I was a little older, Aunt Gioia, our Uncle Tom's wife, would take me out in her car, which had no heater. I don't know whether it was due to the cold or the speed at which my aunt drove, but I would inevitably end up with a nose bleed, which I would try to keep secret, all the while pretending to have tremendous fun as Aunt Gioia swung her car around the bends as though leading the pack in the British Grand Prix.

My own first set of wheels was a heavy old pram that had doubtless conveyed many Owtram babies before me. It had thin metal wheels that rattled horribly over the slightest bump. It wasn't terribly comfortable on a country road but every day my mother or Nanny Kent would push me up and down the local lanes to get some air. Sometimes my mother pushed me all the way into Dolphinholme village, a mile or so away. One day she unwisely set off, with me on board, down the steep path connecting the upper and lower halves of the village, which was called Livestock Hill, and the pram – which had no brake – started to run away with her.

As the pram gathered speed, my mother had to sprint to keep up with it. Faster and faster we went, with no sign whatsoever that my mother was about to regain control.

'Isn't this fun, Pat!' she gasped as we careered towards what might well have been a fatal collision with a gate and fence at the bottom of the slope.

'Not at all, it isn't fun,' I replied gloomily.

Somehow we avoided a disaster, but I was always wary of pram rides that went via Livestock Hill after that.

When I was two years old, my mother became pregnant again and, as she entered the later stages of her pregnancy, it was decided that I would go to stay with Nanny Kent at her own home for a while. It was no hardship for me. I adored Nanny Kent and loved staying with her at her house in Coronation Villas in Smarden, near Ashford in Kent (hence her nickname), among the bright green hop gardens for which the local area was famous.

While I was there, Nanny Kent dutifully kept my mother informed with regard to my well-being and daily activities. Nanny Kent's 'budget', as she called the diary which she sent back to Newland Hall each week, documents a very busy time for Baby Pat – making mud pies and visiting the hop gardens. According to Nanny Kent, I was also a keen church-goer, having evolved somewhat from the 'wailing babe' who required special prayers to keep her quiet through the sermon. Nanny Kent wrote: 'Pat asks every day if it is Sunday and can she go to church. I always ask her if she wants to go for a walk with me or to Church and she always says "Church".' Nanny Kent thought it might be the prospect of singing hymns that interested me, rather than my having any particular ecclesiastical bent.

One day, Nanny Kent and I met the vicar's wife on a walk. She leaned down towards me and said, 'I hope Pat that you always say your prayers.'

I told her proudly, 'I say "thank you, God" every time I see a star.' It was an absolute fib but the vicar's wife seemed happy.

During the same stay there were visits to the sea-side at Hythe (presumably Nanny Kent kept her hat and black coat on, whatever the weather) and also to the nearby aerodrome at Lympne, where I was transfixed by an aerobatic display. We picked juicy ripe blackberries from the hedgerows and collected grass to feed to the pigs on a neighbouring farm. I remember visiting a litter of little brown and mauve piglets. There were kittens to play with too and I made a friend in the shape of Nanny Kent's niece, a slightly older girl called Freda. No wonder when Nanny Kent told me that she would soon be taking me back to Lancashire, I told her flatly that I didn't want to go.

I was only persuaded by the promise of the imminent arrival of a brand-new playmate at Newland Hall. I was going to have a little brother or sister. I was terribly excited as we travelled back to Lancashire, thinking of all the fun I would have with my very own sibling. You can imagine my disappointment then when I was taken along to meet this new sibling for the first time. I was expecting a child of at least my own age, preferably a little older, who could straight away join me in my games, but here was a tiny baby – a little shrimp in a shawl, her face all screwed up with bawling.

'She's much too little to be of any use!' I cried, when I was introduced to my brand-new sister Jean. My parents had ordered the wrong thing and I was very disappointed.

CHAPTER FOUR

Jean

I was born in November 1925, ahead of what was to be a turbulent year for Britain. The economy was faltering and the spring and early summer of 1926 saw a general strike in support of the coal miners, who were themselves striking over the prospect of reduced pay. Almost two million strikers in all the vital industries downed tools in an attempt to force a Government U-turn over the wage reductions. It was the largest industrial dispute in Britain's history, bringing chaos to the nation. The general strike continued for just nine days but the miners were still striking when I turned one. King George V made a rare statement on the situation, saying: 'Try living on their wages before you judge them.'

Of course, I had no idea what sort of world I was coming into. My own earliest memories are, like Pat's, largely based around the family anecdotes and photographs that our mother collected together in the baby book. By the time I was born, with two small children and a house to run, Bunty no longer had time to decorate the pages with her delicate pen and ink drawings, but she continued to take lots of photographs and jotted down her favourite stories. There are several photographs of Pat holding me, aged about six months, on her lap. Pat still seems fairly unimpressed to have a sister. She looks as though she might drop me at any moment.

Gradually, I became more useful as a sibling. Towards the back of the baby book is a sequence of photographs of Pat and me taken in the winter of 1928/29, both wrapped up like Father Christmas' elves against the icy weather. That winter was a particularly harsh one and in February 1929, it got so cold that Lake Windermere in nearby Cumbria froze over. It's quite unusual for a lake of such a size and depth to freeze. Our parents took us to see the rare spectacle and we joined dozens of people on the ice. Our mother wore ice skates. Our father pulled me and Pat along on a toboggan. In the photographs taken that day, I look more than a little nervous as I stand next to Pat on the frozen water, clutching her hand, eyes narrowed as though I'm listening hard for any sign that the ice might be cracking beneath us.

In a photograph taken later that same year, Pat and I stand on the front steps at Newland Hall behind a line-up of our favourite toys, including a large, grumpy looking teddy bear, called Jenny, who is carrying a small bear on her back. The smaller bear was Koko, Pat's favourite. Jenny was mine and she still lives at the bottom of the stairs in my Lancashire cottage.

The following year, 1930, our family grew again. Just as in the weeks before I was born, Nanny Kent stepped in to give our parents time to prepare for the new arrival and Pat and I were taken to Coronation Villas. I found it every bit as interesting to be there as Pat did, enjoying making mud pies in Nanny Kent's garden. Though we had been warned by Nanny Kent to keep out of their way, I was intrigued by the hop pickers, whole families from London – from the grand-parents, right down to the toddlers – who came to Kent for the harvest on a sort of working holiday at the end of the summer. Their Cockney rhyming slang was so different to the way we spoke in Lancashire.

I must have been potty-training during that stay with Nanny Kent because my strongest memory of Coronation Villas is of being sent to sit on a pot that had been posi-tioned in the tiled hallway facing the front door. There was a clear glass panel in the door and I was very happy to be in such a prime position, watching the goings on in the street outside and keeping a look out for visitors. Perhaps I'd catch a glimpse of those interesting hop-pickers…

Once again, Nanny Kent kept our mother informed of our activities with her 'budget'. She writes of sunny days in the garden and tea parties with friends and of visits to church and of Pat telling her over breakfast one day, in a very thoughtful manner:

'When I am grown up I shall have some children, then they will have some children, and I shall bring them all here for you. Perhaps one would have to sleep in the larder, but I don't think that would matter do you?'

After a couple of weeks, we returned home and shortly after that, our little brother Robert – 'Bob' – was born. Pat and I were in the nursery with our cousin Jill when we were called into the front bedroom to see our mother and meet our new sibling. When we found her, our mother was sitting in the bed with baby Robert in her arms. Pat and I had a quick look at him, finding him about as exciting as Pat had first found me – much too small to be of any use – then we rushed to find Jill, who was by now in the bath. Cousin Jill was an only child and we felt rather sorry for her about it. All the same, we couldn't wait to share our news.

'We've got a brother!' we told her triumphantly.

'Poo,' said Jill. 'I wouldn't want one of those.'

I'd gone from being the youngest to being the middle child. All the attention was on Bob now but I was still very enthusiastic about having a brother. As he got older, it meant that I had someone to keep me company, while I was dragging along behind Pat. That said, Pat was a very good big sister to me when we were small. For many years we shared a bedroom just off the nursery, and though we weren't supposed to talk after lights out, each night Pat would make up long stories to tell me as I drifted off to sleep. They often involved an imaginary child called Molly, who got into all sorts of exciting situations and scrapes.

During the day, Pat involved me in elaborate make-believe games that we called 'pretends'. Our pretends, in which we played at being characters from history, could go on for days, becoming ever more elaborate. The Jacobite Rising of 1745 became a favourite theme for play time. We were both fascinated by the story of Bonnie Prince Charlie – the Young Pretender – and loved putting on the eighteenth century-style costumes we found in the dressing up box to act out his story again and again.

We were fortunate to have large gardens to roam in good weather. In the middle of the lawn in front of the house was a pond that seemed to us to be an enormous lake, where we could float in a little rowing boat. But some of my favourite memories of Newland Hall are of playing in the grand entrance hall, with its beautiful red Persian carpet on the polished parquet floor and the imposing grandfather clock standing guard.

Pat and I devised a game that involved lots of running up and down the stairs. Up and down we went again and again and again. Then we graduated to sliding down the bannisters at high speed. We had to be stopped before someone had an accident. Quietly, we moved the game to the back stairs, which led down to the kitchen, where we thought no-one could see us.

By the time Bob arrived, Nanny Kent had all but retired and we were being looked after by Miss Annie Bridges, whom we called 'Nanny BeeBee'. Nanny BeeBee wore glasses and a rather crushed black hat and she taught us a mantra for life, which was that whatever disaster befell one, whether it be bruised knees, cut fingers, blackberry-bush scratches, one must say to oneself 'It might have been very much worse! It might have been very much worse! It might have been very, very much worse!' It didn't matter how badly you thought you were hurt. Even a headlong tumble on the gravel drive was an occasion for the cheery chant.

It might have sounded harsh, particularly as Nanny BeeBee had a rather stern face, but she was very kind and over the years, her advice has proved invaluable. There really are very few things in life that can't be put into perspective with those seven simple words.

'It might have been very much worse!'

CHAPTER FIVE

Pat

It was Nanny BeeBee who taught me how to read the summer I turned four. We would sit in the playroom garden, with Nanny in the low nursing chair and me in a little brown chair alongside her, studying the book on her knees. The playroom garden was so called because a door led directly from it into the long low stone building which had been a cowshed (or shippen as we called it in Lancashire) until our grandfather turned it into a room for dances, and informal concerts, and beaters' lunches on winter shooting days – a 'playroom' for children and adults alike.

That long-ago summer, Nanny BeeBee and I pored over a Victorian book called 'Reading Without Tears', in which the alphabet was represented in pictures. Now, more than 95 years later, I still see the letter A as a little house with one window, B as a little house with two windows, C as a child on a swing. Later in the same book came a series of short stories designed to test the new reader's progress. There was a particularly frightening one about young Fanny, who saved her little brother from being eaten by wolves by hiding him in a cupboard, heroically failing to save herself in the process. For a long time after reading that I was quietly frightened about wolves.

Later on, when our mother read us Rudyard Kipling's stories about India, I became quietly frightened instead that an enormous tiger might creep in through the nursery window and lurk under my bed, ready to pounce the moment I fell asleep. Nanny BeeBee and my parents assured me endlessly that tigers don't usually lurk in rural North Lancashire but I didn't believe them. I remained ever watchful, determined to avoid poor Fanny's grisly fate.

Of course, soon after I learned to read, I learned to write and Nanny made the mistake of letting me compose an addendum to one of her letters to my mother, who was away visiting my maternal grandparents in Bath. My mother saved this earliest example of my prose for posterity. At the bottom of a note regarding my progress in the nursery, which says I am being *extra good*, I scribbled, 'Dear Mummie, I'se writing to say Nannie is not kind to me. She won't let me eat paper…' Very unkind indeed.

Nanny BeeBee taught me to read but it was my mother, who loved reading, who decided when I was born that she would provide a library for me. The first book she bought was 'Three Men In A Boat' by Jerome K. Jerome. I have never discovered whether any more books followed but I know that by the age of four I had begun to compose little poems which I recited to my mother so that she could write them down. That was the beginning of a lifelong interest in poetry.

If our mother never bought another book after 'Three Men In A Boat', it hardly mattered. Newland Hall was full of books, complete sets of the novels of Dickens and Scott in glass-fronted cases, boys' books belonging to our father and his three brothers, the books we exchanged at the Boots Book-Lovers' Library in Lancaster with little shields on their covers, Beatrix Potter and 'The Wind In The Willows' in our nursery. The novels of Dickens and Scott were much too old for me but I read them anyway, lapping up their stories of worlds so different to my own.

A particular childhood favourite of mine was a picture book called 'Les Malheurs Du Sophie' by the Countess de Ségur. The book was written in French and was possibly a gift from our maternal grandmother Agnes, known to us as Gaggie, who was bilingual. At an early age, I had come to know a smattering of French through listening to her talking with my mother. They would switch from English to French when they were discussing things that weren't suitable for our young ears. Gaggie also often read to us in her mother tongue and I believe that hearing books in French when we were small gave me and Jean an advantage when it came to learning other languages later on.

'Les Malheurs De Sophie' (Sophie's Misfortunes) was first published in 1858 and it was set in the time of the Second French Empire. The heroine, the high-spirited Sophie de Réan, lived with her parents in a castle in the countryside. Despite the best efforts of her friends to keep her on the straight and narrow, the constitutionally reckless Sophie was always getting into terrible scrapes.

As a young girl, I was entranced by the tale, listening in fascinated horror as Sophie lurched from one disaster to the next. It seemed that the harder she tried to be good, the worse things became. I must have felt I knew how hard it was to be good, writing this list of resolutions in my diary at around the same time as 'Les Malheurs De Sophie' became my best-loved bedtime story:

1. *Always do as Jesus would have done.*
2. *Read the Bible each day.*
3. *Keep diary.*
4. *Always love Jean.*
5. *Always have good manners.*
6. ~~*See if I can be good.*~~ *See if this can be the best year I've lived.*

I obviously wasn't optimistic about my chances of being good!

Each night, our parents told us stories before we went to sleep. When I was very young, I only wanted my father to tell the stories and they had to be on one of two themes: stories about a diver, and stories about how they built the road from Preston to Lancaster. Daddy told and retold several variations on this limited repertoire. Later our mother took over and told us two different stories every evening: one would be about fairies, and the other what we called a 'good story' – a Christian one. We were raised as Protestant Christians, the faith firmly held by our family. In our nursery was a 'Good Table', decorated with a blue cloth and a wooden crucifix and a cardboard cut-out of the Baby Jesus, on which we put flowers from the garden.

Those 'good stories' were actually often awful tales about the persecution of the early Christians that inspired Jean to declare one bedtime, 'Thank goodness, Mummy, that we aren't Christians.'

According to our mother, I piped up with a simple solution to the early Christians' problems. 'Why didn't they pretend they weren't Christians and just be Christians on the inside?'

In those early years of our childhood, Newland Hall was still very much Grandboffin's domain. Our parents were always kind and interested in our likes and dislikes and our childhood was certainly not of the 'seen and not heard' variety – in fact, we were for the most part treated like small adults – but Grandboffin liked his home to be run in the Edwardian fashion, familiar to anyone who has ever watched 'Upstairs, Downstairs'.

At that time it was usual for children of the upper classes to spend most of their lives in the nursery. They were only allowed downstairs for so long and were especially not to interrupt work in the kitchen. Jean and I loved to spend time in the kitchen. We were always thrilled when we were invited to visit the servants' hall to have tea with the cook, the housemaid and the parlourmaid, not knowing how, in the years to come, evenings spent in the servants' hall would have such an impact on our lives.

CHAPTER SIX

Jean

In the 1920s any large house would have a number of permanent staff and Newland Hall was no exception. At one point, the house had quite a large staff – the 1921 census suggests as many as seven – but by the time Pat and I came along, that number had dwindled to a cook and two maids.

Ellen Isaacs was the housemaid. Her role was to keep the house clean and tidy, which can't have been easy with three children and various dogs constantly bringing in the mud. She hoovered, dusted and laid the fires each morning. She polished the floors and the dark wooden furniture that decorated every room.

One day, our mother asked her, 'didn't you ought to dust the bannisters, Ellen.' It was evident that she'd missed them out.

'I did,' Ellen responded.

'Oh,' said our mother, still admiring a layer of dust thick enough to write her name in. 'You did?'

'No, I did *ought* to,' said Ellen.

Each morning, Ellen brought brass jugs of warm water to wash in to each of the bedrooms. This became known to us children as 'Ellen water'. Though we often complained that it was lukewarm by the time it got to us, it was no small task for Ellen to lug that water around the house before everyone woke up.

Years later, I came to understand just how hard Ellen worked when, aged 18 and keen to do my bit in the war, I joined the First Aid Nursing Yeomanry. My basic training for the FANY took place in a requisitioned country house with what seemed like an impossible number of fireplaces. The first job of each and every morning was to clean all the grates and lay fires for the evening. I was worn out before I even got to breakfast. It made me appreciate all the more everything that Ellen had done for us.

Ellen left our family's employ in 1939 to get married. According to the census, she became a 'raincoat cleaner', which must have seemed like a relief after all those years of carrying 'Ellen water' up and down the stairs.

As a parlourmaid, Eva's role was more public-facing. Wearing a smart black uniform with a starched white apron, her job was to let visitors into the house and to serve afternoon tea, which was a meal of some ritual.

Unfortunately, Eva was not always quite as discreet as she might have been when it came to receiving visitors. One afternoon, unexpected guests came to call on our mother. Since our mother was not in the mood to entertain, thinking she would rather take a walk around the woods than make small talk with uninvited callers, she instructed Eva, 'Tell them that I'm out.'

Eva promptly returned to the people waiting patiently in the hallway and announced in a loud voice, while our mother listened in horror from her hiding place at the top of the stairs, 'Mrs Owtram says she's out.'

Perhaps our mother shouldn't have been surprised at Eva's lack of tact. Lancashire people in those days were cheerful, plain-dealing, and took pride in speaking the truth. A bride from another part of the country was startled, after her first appearance in our local church, to be greeted by her husband's neighbours with hearty handshakes and the comment, 'You married a plain man, Mrs E!' She had no idea that 'plain' in Lancashire means 'honest' and she was receiving the highest compliment.

I'm sure our mother was very embarrassed by Eva's honesty with the unwanted visitors that afternoon. She and our father believed in doing the right thing and fibbing to callers would not seem to fall within that category. Our parents taught us always to act with integrity within the family and within the wider community. They were both very involved with the local church. Our father was a church warden. Our mother was responsible for the flowers that decorated the nave every Sunday. She also played a key part in the local Mothers' Union.

The Mothers' Union was affiliated to the Church of England and its purpose was to promote marriage and family life, encouraging its members to raise their children in the Christian faith. Our mother was the 'enrolling member' of the Dolphinholme branch of the MU, which met every month for an inspiring talk, usually about the C of E's charity work and overseas missions. Our mother was very good at giving talks and was in demand at neighbouring unions as a visiting speaker. There were also regular Mothers' Union teas and fetes, which involved a great deal of organisation.

Another of the Mothers' Union duties was to visit local people suffering from ill health. Our mother diligently visited anybody who was unwell and helped them in any way she could. She really cared about people and in an unofficial way, always did as much as she was able to improve the lives of those around her.

Whereas these days one might meet a friend in a coffee shop, it was the custom in the '20s and '30s to call on people at their houses. As the eldest daughter in the family, Pat was expected to carry on the tradition, so our mother would often take Pat with her on calls. Pat didn't need to be asked twice. She loved having the opportunity to visit other houses. Her favourite thing was to be invited to look around a house, particularly if the lady of the house allowed her a peek in her wardrobe. If that was in the offing, Pat would be up like a rabbit.

I was less interested in clothes, but as children we did have some beautiful dresses. As well as being a talented artist, our mother was a skilled seamstress and knitter, trained in dressmaking by the nuns who taught at her school in Preston. She knitted our father's socks (I didn't inherit her talent for knitting, taking a whole term to make a single sock for the war effort when asked to do so at school). Our mother made our jerseys and also sewed smocks and summer dresses. We loved the summer dresses she made for us using cotton from

Horrockses – the mill where Grandboffin was a director for many years. They were always very intricately smocked around the bodice. In later life, our mother would put her dressmaking skills to work again when she opened her own dress shop in Garstang.

With her passion for fashion, Pat dreamed of having her own walk-in wardrobe and often doodled elegantly-dressed models in the margins of her diaries. She was most put out to miss the opportunity to be bridesmaid – and wear the commensurate fancy dress – when our Uncle Godfrey married our neighbours' daughter Joan Gardiner, who had been our mother's bridesmaid. Together with our cousin Jill, who was closer to me in age, I was Joan's bridesmaid, while Pat was given the less prestigious role of flower girl. Pat was very envious of our specially-made gold dresses (I couldn't have cared less what I was wearing). We were led up the aisle by Nanny BeeBee, while Pat followed behind with a basket of artificial rose petals. Pat was allowed to wear a new dress of her own but it wasn't gold and I remember she was still peeved.

While Pat was following in the footsteps of our mother, I spent much more time with Grandboffin. With his four sons all grown and our little brother Bob still too small to help out on the farm, I stepped into the role that might usually have fallen to a grandson. Fortunately, like Grandboffin, I was very fond of animals and was only too happy to keep him company while he tended to his livestock.

Grandboffin was very much involved in the farm at

Newland, where he had 90 acres stocked with pigs, poultry, a pedigree flock of Leicester Longwool sheep and a pedigree herd of Dairy Shorthorn cows, of which he was especially proud. I learned a great deal from following my grandfather and his farm bailiff about their work. I was thrilled to overhear Grandboffin telling one of his friends, when I was a small girl, that I had the shoulders of a farmer. It seemed like the best sort of compliment. Farmers were people I greatly admired.

I very much enjoyed going to the country shows and walking Grandboffin's favourite shorthorn cows around the parade ring. True to their breed, they were always good and docile when it came to their turn in the spotlight, seeming to understand that they needed to be on their best behaviour on a show day. There was never any trouble persuading the cows into the trailer that would take them to the show ground either. In fact, they rather seemed to enjoy the opportunity to get out and about. The cows all had names. One of my favourites was Newland Rose. She was a particularly successful show cow, bringing home lots of trophies. Our sheep often won awards too.

I have always loved animals. As a child, if I was feeling sad or lonely, I would confide in the nearest dog. I loved the way they always seemed to listen carefully to my problems and offer comfort with their gentle eyes. To this day, I much prefer dogs to people! We had a variety of dogs at Newland. There were spaniels, Labradors and a Dandie Dinmont called Meg, who was added to the pack in the hope of encouraging Pat to be more confident around the family pets.

One of my favourite dogs was a spaniel called Sam, who was officially 'my dog'. Sam was actually acquired as a replacement for another dog, also called Sam, a much-loved puppy who died suddenly while on a walk. Shortly afterwards, our parents went on holiday to Scotland and there met a family called the Mackies who had a puppy uncannily like the one I was mourning. The family had a new baby and were persuaded to let the puppy go back to Newland at a price. I'll never forget the joy of welcoming Sam number two into our home.

Our mother wrote about it in her diary: 'Jean is delighted with Sam and he has settled down well and galumphs around Meg – not too pleased to see him at first!'

I have since had many lovely dogs in my life, most recently a rescue pup. We were in many ways the perfect match but after I had a fall and had to spend some time recovering in a residential home, I realised that it wouldn't be fair to keep him any longer and regretfully passed him on to a family who could make sure he got the exercise he needed. I miss having a dog of my own very much, so I'm always glad to say 'hello' to any pup I might meet on my daily walk.

CHAPTER SEVEN

Jean

If the interior of Newland Hall was the domain of women, the building itself and the grounds around it were the province of the men. The gardens and the immediate environs of the house were kept by a number of gardeners and handymen led by Tommy Townson, who lived in the grounds in a cottage called The Bothy.

Tommy Townson came from Kendal in the Lake District. As a young man, he had served in the Army during the Great War. His role was that of a 'batman', a personal servant to a commissioned officer. An officer's batman was in charge of the officer's kit and also, when horses were still used in combat – such as they were in the Great War – the batman had responsibility for his officer's horse.

During his time in the army, Townson had suffered a great misfortune, though not at the hands of the enemy. While serving on the Western Front, he had to sleep in a tent with a number of other men. In the freezing winter weather, the tent was kept warm by a stove that put out terrible fumes. To keep the fumes from getting into their sleeping quarters, the soldiers hung blankets around the stove as make-shift curtains. Unfortunately during the night, the blankets fell down and Townson and his colleagues inhaled toxic smoke as they slept. Several of the men became ill. Townson was left with a disabling lung condition that necessitated his return to civilian life.

Townson's role at Newland Hall was varied. Each morning, he would drive our father and Grandboffin to the local station, where they would catch the train to Preston where our family mill – Cliff Mill – was situated. Every evening, he would be there to pick them up again.

While our father and Grandboffin were at their offices, Townson would return to Newland and set about the usual maintenance tasks required at such a large house. He took care of the temperamental boiler. He made sure the family cars were always in tip top condition and sparkling clean. He also looked after our father's beautiful horse, Sandy.

Our father was a keen rider and he would take Sandy out every morning before leaving for work. Some days, he would ride as far as the coast, five miles away, before breakfast. On his way back, he would always stop beneath the nursery window and Pat and I, who had heard Sandy clip-clopping around to our side of the house, would jump up and run to the window to pass down sugar-lumps, saved from tea-time, for Sandy to crunch between his big teeth.

Townson also looked after Dolly, the pony given to me and Pat one Christmas by our Great-Aunt Flo. Aunt Flo had cleverly married Lord Ashton, a local businessman who had made a fortune in linoleum and whose money she dispensed with great largesse. We were very excited to be given such a wonderful gift. The whole family gathered on the verandah to meet the new addition to our family. Pat was the first to ride Dolly but didn't get very far before she was thrown off and landed badly. After that, she never quite trusted Dolly again. I was a more natural horse-woman and eagerly looked forward to riding Dolly around the lanes each day after lessons, while Townson rode his bicycle alongside to make sure that I didn't come to any harm.

Dolly was a rather unpredictable pony but she gave me a good introduction to riding. Together she and I were the toast of The Pony Club. Whenever Dolly felt like behaving, that is. I've continued to love riding horses my whole life and, thanks to my friend Clare, was lucky enough to have the opportunity to do some riding during an easing in the Covid lockdown in the summer of 2020. Though it had been a while, and it wasn't as easy to get into the saddle at 95 years of age as it had been back when I was nine, I felt very happy to be spending time around horses again.

Tommy Townson was a very important part of the Newland team. He was a bachelor. He never married and he had no children. He remained in the cottage at Newland Hall until he retired at around 70 years of age, at which point he went to live at The Fleece Inn, half a mile from the house on the corner between Dolphinholme and Bay Horse, where he was very well looked after.

The formal gardens at Newland Hall, which had been designed and put in place by our great-grandmother, needed constant attention. Our great-grandmother loved rhododendrons and planted many flower beds. However, due to the nature of the land around the house, which had been reclaimed from the boggy moors, unwanted plants such as heather and rushes were always threatening to push their way through her elegant lawns.

The chief gardener at Newland during our childhood was Murphy. He hailed from Ireland and, like Townson, lived in a cottage on the estate. He was assisted by a gardener's boy – Walter Hodgson – who arrived in the 1930s. When war was declared, Walter insisted that he couldn't be called up, because he considered himself an essential food producer.

Away from the formal gardens, which led down to a round pond where we loved to paddle a small rowing boat in the summer, there were woodlands to be managed too. The largest part was called Wellington Wood, so-named because it was planted during the Napoleonic Wars of the early 19th century, when Arthur Wellesley, 1st Duke of Wellington, soldier and twice prime minister, led the British troops to a famous victory over Napoleon at the Battle of Waterloo.

The woods were home to many birds and animals, including pheasants raised for shooting. Every Saturday during the pheasant season, which ran from October to the beginning of February, our father and grandfather and other local landowners would take it in turns to host shooting parties on their various estates. Men from the village were recruited as 'beaters', walking ahead of the 'guns' to flush out the game from the woods. I will always remember the sound of the men's hob-nailed boots rattling on the cobbles as they arrived in the farmyard, where they would gather before setting off. Depending on the time of year, the hunters also shot rabbits, hares and partridges.

As girls, Pat and I were not expected to hunt, but from time to time we did have to walk behind the guns and help to carry the dead game back to the house. It was not a pleasant task.

After the shoot, the beaters were invited to lunch in the playroom, that old barn which Grandboffin had converted and fitted with wood-burners and a sprung floor, while the invited 'guns' ate in the dining room of the house. At the end of the day, everyone took home some of the day's game for the pot.

At other times of the year, our father hunted rabbits with ferrets. The ferrets lived in cages in the orchard and gave off a terrible whiff. It's hard to imagine that the rabbits didn't smell them coming. I felt very sorry for them. As Pat used to say: 'Any animal should be safe in its own burrow.' I tend to agree with her.

But the ferrets didn't only flush out those poor rabbits. Part of the Newland Hall estate comprised a hill, covered by woodland. Many years ago when our father and some other people were looking for rabbits there, they lost a ferret down a hole and began to dig it out. As they dug, they uncovered a strange oblong pit the size of an adult human grave, lined with slabs of stone, and with a stone lying like a bridge across the top of it. Nearby lay two other large flat stones, evidently meant to fit over the hollow as covers. It was a most surprising discovery.

The pit was eventually identified as an ancient sacrificing-place built by members of the mysterious Cult of Mithras.

It lay on the eastward slope of the hill, facing the Pennines, and it's thought that at the moment the sun rose over their crest, the cult's priest would sacrifice an animal laid on the bridge-slab so that its blood would drip onto a worshipper lying in the pit underneath in a rite of purification. In most representations of the god, Mithras is shown slaughtering a bull, a potent symbol of vitality, to release its energy for the good of mankind.

We often wondered who they were, these people who once lived on the hilltop in our woods? The origins of the Mithraic cult are obscure but it seems to have been introduced into Britain by the Romans, so perhaps there was a Roman outpost on the crest of the hill guarding the approaches to the road down below, along which the legions and chariots passed with shields and spears glinting in the sun, to and from the great camp on the Lune. The hill is an excellent lookout point − no nation ever had a keener eye for the strategic use of a country than the Romans. One cannot travel far about England without realising this.

Possibly, though, these worshippers of Mithras were not the Romans, nor even their native conscripts, but some local tribe who had learnt about the cult from the invaders and who, after the legions had been pulled back again towards Rome, practised the mystery on a hillside that had become merely part of the lonely, forested, marshy country again. Whoever they were, we are not likely to learn much about them now − unless someone new one day excavates the curious bumps and hollows there still are on that hilltop and finds that it holds more secrets.

Grandboffin often welcomed archaeologists interested in the site to Newland Hall. The archaeologists all had their theories about our magical cave but as children we much preferred the fanciful stories we created with our own imaginations. The Lune Valley has always had a mystical feel to it. At Newland, one would wake to the sound of the farmyard cock crowing. Our cock would set off the cock on the next farm and then the next and the next and the next. It seemed a very ancient sound, that crowing; unchanged through the centuries. How lucky we were to grow up in such a timeless landscape, living in tune with the seasons as did the many generations who lived there before us.

CHAPTER EIGHT

Pat

During our childhood, a great number of cooks went through the kitchen at Newlands. Kitchen maids also came and went with alarming frequency. I remember the day that Kitty the kitchen maid ran away, pursued down the driveway by the cook Mrs Mason, waving her arms (possibly brandishing a spoon) and shouting at the top of her voice. It was quite the spectacle. Jean and I were fascinated to see the drama unfold from our viewpoint at an upstairs window. Mrs Mason didn't catch up with Kitty and we never saw the kitchen maid again.

The cook had special status in the house and was always referred to as 'Mrs', to reflect her importance, but finding and keeping good cooks was quite the endeavour. Many of the letters that flew between our mother and our Aunt Gioia in the '30s dwell on the subject. Each new hiring meant an anxious wait to see whether cooking was actually in the new incumbent's repertoire of skills.

When there was a cook in the house, our mother would announce that it was time to eat in her own inimitable way. She would sit down at the piano and play a song entitled 'Soup of the Evening'. It was the mock turtle's song from Lewis Carroll's 'Alice in Wonderland'. As soon as we heard those words – 'Soup of the evening, beautiful soup' – we would run to find out what was on the day's menu.

As small children, we did not eat with the adults – we ate at a table in the nursery – and the meals the cook prepared for us were very different from those that were served in the dining room. Nursery meals were generally very bland. I remember eating an awful lot of white fish in plain white sauce. Good for the brain.

There was always a pudding but alas puddings were rarely all that exciting either. They consisted of an endless round of sago, semolina and tapioca – despised by most children, including us, for its uncanny similarity to frog spawn. It was all perfectly flavourless, to match the white fish. One of our least favourite desserts was junket – milk made solid with rennet. No-one would dream of eating such a horrible thing now. We would long for syrup pudding or as a very special treat, a sort of sticky toffee pudding made from bread dipped in a syrup mixture and fried. That was worth finishing one's fish for.

Rice pudding often made an appearance on the menu. If it made it up the stairs… Our mother once happened across Ellen the housemaid scraping something off the carpet in the hall. When she asked what it was, Ellen explained that it was the rice pudding the cook had prepared for the children's supper. It was clear that she had intended to scoop it back into the dish and carry on up to the nursery, thinking we wouldn't notice. Thankfully, on that occasion, our mother was able to intervene.

There was a brief wonderful moment when the puddings

that came out of the kitchen at Newland Hall were particularly good. That was when Edith Krochmalnik of Vienna was at the helm. Unfortunately, the apfelstrudel and Weiner torta that were such a hit with us children, were not to Grandboffin's liking – they were far too exotic – and he soon made sure that only bland English puddings were on the menu again. Still, the food served downstairs was always better and Jean and I always looked forward to Sundays when a roast lunch might at least be followed by an apple pie or dumplings or a crumble of some sort.

There is one Sunday lunch, when I was allowed to eat with the adults, that particularly sticks in my mind. I was about six years old. Our parents had invited the local vicar to join us. Dressed in my Sunday best, I took my place at the table next to him. It was so exciting. I was very much looking forward to finding out what sort of things the adults talked about while I was stuck upstairs with Jean and Nanny BeeBee. You can imagine my disappointment then when the Vicar leaned towards me and, in lieu of the interesting and erudite conversation I had hoped for, he started to make strange animal noises.

'Moo, Pat, moo!' he said. Then, 'Baa, Pat, baaaaa!'

I was mortified on his behalf. What was the vicar trying to say? Had he suddenly lost the ability to speak? I did not know how I ought to respond so I decided that my best course of action was to say nothing and concentrate on the food in front of me. I remained stony-faced, with my eyes firmly on my plate, while the vicar continued to moo and baa at me throughout the meal, seemingly undaunted by my lack of response.

When lunch was over and our guests were all gone, my mother took me to one side and said, 'You weren't very friendly to the vicar today, Pat. Why weren't you nicer when he made all those funny noises for you?'

I told her, 'I thought it was kinder to pretend not to notice the unfortunate man.'

Later that same year, my mother took Jean and I on a short break to a guest-house at the seaside somewhere between Fleetwood and Blackpool, where we met up with her parents, Pops and Gaggie. The owner of the guest-house was one Mrs Raby, a curious woman who had a habit of wiping her mouth before speaking, as though sweeping away a cobweb. Her adult daughter did the same. It rained every day of that holiday, I remember, and the tide was always either out of sight or flooding the promenade.

Just as in the nursery at home, food at the guest house was a daily source of disappointment. Mrs Raby's only pudding was rice, which we had every day enlivened with jam. And when our mother asked if we might have fishcakes one evening, Mrs Raby replied that she didn't do fancy cooking, though when Uncle Herbert and Aunt Doll came to join us for lunch, Mrs Raby pulled out the stops and I had asparagus (sparrow-grass) for the very first time.

Upstairs I shared a back-bedroom with our mother, which looked on to a run of skinny hens, to which we threw crumbs. I would have thrown them my rice pudding if I thought I might get away with it. I remember there was a picture of 'The Flight into Egypt' in the bedroom, which impressed me very much. There were pictures of tame swans on lakes in the dining room which seemed vast to me in 1930: these enchanted Jean, who was about a yard high then.

It seems now as though we stayed with Mrs Raby for ages, though it can't have been the case. I remember Jean remarking: 'Pop's hair is awfully short, Mummy, isn't it? P'raps it hasn't growed yet.' And I got my bicycle – my seventh birthday present – there, and crashed it against the gatepost. The bathroom was at the end of a long passage, and it always seemed to be occupied by a shadowy presence – another lodger. This annoyed BeeBee, our nanny at the time, very much. There also Gaggie got rheumatic fever and nearly died.

Not a particularly successful holiday then. Thank goodness there were better trips, particularly to Blair Atholl in Perthshire, where the Scottish landscape captured our hearts (and the food was very much better). Some of the happiest moments of our childhood were spent in the Highlands; learning to fish alongside our father, watching for the trout to rise at dusk or just sitting quietly side by side outside our rented cottage, looking out for the flare of the Northern Lights.

CHAPTER NINE

Jean

Many of my early memories are linked to Dolphinholme's Memorial Hall, which had once been the mill warehouse. All parish events took place there including Sunday School parties, when each child was given a newly minted 6d. from the Garnett Bequest in addition to a large tea; and the fancy dress parade when rain washed out the sports day. There were splendid village concerts with much local talent, some of which is indelibly etched in my memory, like Billy Driver (the local 'Wolf') singing 'What're yer goin'ter do abaht Selina?' (who'd broken his heart and the sofa springs), the robust Harold Harrison, who farmed Croft Height, performing 'Wiv me little spade and bucket in me 'and', and numerous emotional recitations. I remember dancing the Lancers there, with the floor quivering like a trampoline, and an iron stove slowly turning red hot behind a flimsy railing in one corner, with paper streamers fluttering above it. That seemed more than a little dangerous. The stairs were wooden and there was no other exit from the tall rickety building! In the rather primitive lavatories was a notice saying: 'A time and place for everything, and everything in its time and place'.

Being off the main road, our village was always very much of an entity and devised its own entertainments. The annual sports and flower-and-vegetable show was the main event of the year. The sports, held in a green pasture beside the river, would start with the crowning of an excited but solemn, pink-cheeked little schoolgirl as Rose Queen, continue with races of all kinds the for older children (for prizes of sixpence and threepence) and with other events for their elders such as the slow Cumberland-style wrestling bouts and the sheepdog trials (slender, wonderfully intelligent, wonderfully obedient little black-and-white collies working a bunch of sheep through a gap made with hurdles into the narrow entrance of the pen). The day would finish with a dance in the evening.

All year round, church was at the heart of village life. We attended the Anglican parish church of St Mark but there was also a Methodist chapel – the 'tin chapel' – made of yellow and red corrugated iron. There was always a happy relationship between the two congregations and we staggered the Harvest Festivals so that everyone could go to both. In my earliest childhood I can also just remember an old lady, wearing a black Quaker bonnet, with its deep face-obscuring brim, who drove down to Dolphinholme from nearby Quernmore in a pony trap, and addressed us as 'thou' – the formal second person singular, not the everyday 'dust tha knaw' of 1920's rural Lancashire. The Quaker Meeting Houses at Abbeystead and Quernmore were still in use then, and a famous piece of local history was the story of the Quaker, Mrs Crag, who walked from Ortner in Wyresdale the 250 miles to London during the plague to fetch home her grandchildren.

We were all christened at St Mark's: me, Pat and Bob. As was traditional at the time, Pat and I had two godmothers and one godfather each, while Bob had two godfathers and one godmother. Pat's godfather was our mother's brother, Uncle Charles, known to us as Uncle Tid, which derived from his childhood nickname of 'Tiddler'. Uncle Tid was in the navy and was unable to attend the christening because he was away at sea. He sent a Swedish enamel napkin ring as a christening gift. One of Bob's godfathers was Neil Sandeman, scion of the port, sherry and brandy importers. A very useful godfather indeed.

My godmothers were Aunt Marjorie, our mother's brother's wife, and Aunt Nell Herman, from Sussex. We would often go to stay with the Hermans, who had a lovely house near Brighton, during the summer holidays. Their next-door neighbour was one Lady Lowther and she had a beaver dam on her estate. We were always delighted to spot one of those curious creatures in her garden.

Duly christened, Pat and I attended Sunday School, where we engaged in various bible-related projects and learned about the missionaries, whose work I always found very inspiring. Inside the church we had a family pew near the front of the nave, where we would join our parents for the service.

While we tried to concentrate on the sermon, our little brother Bob would spend most of the time leaning over the back of our pew into the one behind, where usually sat Dora Gort, a local farmer's daughter. Though Dora was three years Bob's senior, he was madly in love with her from the first moment he laid eyes on her. As far as Bob was concerned, the lovely Dora was very much the best thing about Sundays.

Bob's infatuation with Dora was of great interest – and amusement – to the whole family. Among the letters our mother saved was one she had sent to our maternal grandmother Gaggie in Bath, when Bob was around five years old. Describing the weekend's activities, our mother wrote:

I went to early service... then Miss C and Bob and I went to the next, but alas! Again Dora was not there! However Bobbie leant over into the pew behind and whispered to Mrs Gort, her mother, "Do you know when Dora's birthday is?" and was quite contented when she told him!

We were all rooting for Bob and his great first love affair, though I do wonder if Dora ever noticed Bob's total and utter devotion.

Our beloved little brother could always make us laugh. As a child, Bob had three voices. The first was his 'drawing room voice', the received pronunciation which he used with our parents and visitors. Then he had a voice which he used with the local children in the village, copying their Lancashire accents to blend in when he joined in their games. Finally, he had an excellent Scottish accent, learned from his Scottish nanny, Nana Mackenzie. When he said, 'I'm waitin' on you,' he could sound exactly like her.

As Bob was four and a half years younger than me and almost eight years younger than Pat, we tended to indulge him, particularly in the matter of Father Christmas. Bob was still a believer long after Pat and I understood that it was really our parents who left the gifts we found in our stockings on Christmas morning but, as good sisters, we kept up the pretence to humour him. I can remember when Bob started to be a little sceptical about the man in the red coat himself but that same year he excitedly called me and Pat into the billiard room on Christmas morning to inspect a dirty smudge on the floor next to the fireplace.

'It's Father Christmas's sooty foot!' he declared and the magic was preserved for another 12 months.

One year, however, Santa Claus did not arrive as expected. Our mother wrote to Gaggie in Bath to tell her about the incident. The Welches were family friends, who lived in a house called Hampson, in nearby Galgate. Their children Joy and Philip were close in age to Pat and I, so we often spent time together, going to each other's houses for tea and playing long games of tennis on their soggy court in the summer. Mummy wrote:

Well, the Welches gave a very successful party yesterday, and after tea when we were all assembled in the "West Room", Margaret clapped her hands and said, "Children, Santa Claus has not come himself this year etc etc (the usual permissible fabrications of the truth) but he has sent a magic carpet. Now you must all join hands and sing, "We want a magic carpet" and see what happens." So we all joined hands and sang and sang, until the door opened and Joy and Philip appeared in fancy dress in the midst of a decorated toy farm, on a magic carpet covered in presents. It was very nicely done. Bob thoroughly enjoyed it all and wasn't a scrap shy. Then the girls went off to church and rehearsed the nativity play.

Christmas was one of our favourite times of the year at Newland Hall. Each year, we would choose a tree from Wellington Wood to grace the front hall or the billiard room and decorate it with baubles collected through the years.

On Christmas Eve, a group of singers from the village would always come to serenade us with carols in return for a few crowns. I remember how one year our father muffled himself up in coat, hat and scarf – making sure to obscure his face – and knocked on the front door, pretending to be a member of the village choir. He sang his carols beautifully then took his leave without admitting to his identity. Having crept back into the house afterwards, he casually asked Grandboffin if the carol singers had been any good that evening.

Grandboffin told him, 'I only gave the last chap half a crown. He couldn't sing and he smelled of drink.'

There was much amusement when our father revealed that he was the 'tuneless' singer and, as for smelling of drink, he swore he hadn't touched a drop! I think now that Grandboffin was in on the joke.

Christmas Day itself was always a formal occasion. First thing in the morning, we would hurry to church, knowing that we would not be allowed to open our Christmas presents until after the service.

When we got back to the house, we'd find our gifts arranged

in little piles on the billiard table. There were stockings too, filled by Father Christmas as he visited Newland Hall on his whistle-stop world tour.

In the evening, we would dress in our very best clothes – dinner jackets for the gentlemen and long dresses for the ladies – for Christmas dinner. There was always turkey with all the trimmings and a fine Christmas pudding, which would be doused in brandy and brought to the table with a crown of flames. Crackers would be pulled and paper crowns worn.

After dinner, there would be games and more carols. Our mother would play the piano while our father led the singing. Despite Grandboffin's scathing review of the mystery carol singer, our father had a very fine voice.

Then it was back to the nursery for us children, taking time to admire our new toys as we got ready for bed. Our stockings always contained tangerines and other small items but when we were young, in the run-up to Christmas Eve, Pat and I would pore over the Harrods catalogue, in the hope that Father Christmas might think we had been good enough for a really special present. One year, we were very lucky and received from Harrods a toy kitchenette with a miniature dresser that contained a perfect set of proper china plates and cups, and cutlery. The Christmas that beautiful kitchenette arrived felt like a very good one indeed.

CHAPTER TEN

Pat

A gift from Harrods seemed the very height of luxury to us children growing up in rural Lancashire. The magnificent London department store held a special spot in our affections and was top on the list of places we wanted to see whenever we visited our relatives in the capital. Harrods was enormous and sold everything one could imagine and more besides. There was absolutely nothing to compare in Lancaster. Luckily for us, our father's older brother Uncle Tom lived in Belgravia, in Kinnerton Street, and Harrods was practically his corner shop.

Our Uncle Tom was married to Aunt Gioia, a glamorous Anglo-Italian. Gioia was the daughter of the writer and publisher Grant Richards, who launched the careers of such notable authors as George Bernard Shaw, A.E. Houseman, Samuel Butler and James Joyce.

Her mother was the gloriously named Elisina Palamidessi de Castelvecchio, great-great-granddaughter of Napoleon's younger brother Louis. Taking after her father, Aunt Gioia became a writer, publishing a number of popular and well-reviewed novels under the name Anne Stretton. She also had a variety of pen-names under which she wrote serials for various magazines. As children, we weren't allowed to read Aunt Gioia's books but I always found her choice of career fascinating and listened very carefully when she talked about her work.

Not only was Aunt Gioia a successful novelist, she was exceptionally stylish and always dressed in the most up-to-date fashions. She looked particularly dashing in her trademark bespoke tweeds. One city newspaper referred to her as 'the best-dressed woman in London'. She had an eye for the finer things in life and knew exactly where to go to see and be seen. Our Uncle Godfrey, somewhat less reverently, said of his sister-in-law, 'Gioia would rather have a WC in W1 than a mansion in W6.'

Uncle Tom and Aunt Gioia loved to throw glamorous parties, attended by an eclectic group of guests. I remember once being invited to join such a party while I was staying at Kinnerton Street during the school holidays. As she planned the guest list, Aunt Gioia told me in a conspiratorial sort of way, 'We must have Count So-and-So. Count So-and-So always makes the most amusing remarks in French.'

It was a throwaway comment but it left me terrified that I would find myself in conversation with the witty count and have no idea when I was supposed to laugh, my French not quite being up to scratch. Staying with Aunt Gioia, one was always on one's best behaviour and I didn't want to disappoint her with a mis-timed giggle. When the charming count arrived, I found myself completely mute with anxiety at the thought of saying the exact wrong thing at the wrong time.

Aunt Gioia did her very best to civilise me and Jean and,

wanting to be just like her when I grew up, I was keen to observe goings-on in London's high society. However, staying at the house on Kinnerton Street was not all witty counts and impromptu lessons in etiquette.

Jean and I were good friends with Aunt Gioia and Uncle Tom's daughter, our cousin Jill, who was often sent to Newland Hall in the holidays so that Aunt Gioia could finish a book in writerly peace. Jill was a little younger than both of us but she and I got on especially well and together we had some wonderful adventures. A true city child, Jill had far more freedom in London than Jean and I had in rural Lancashire. In many ways, she was left to her own devices. When I was in London, I was awarded the same freedoms.

One of Jill's favourite things was to play a riotous game of 'hide and seek' in Harrods. Whenever Aunt Gioia took us to the store, Jill and I would do our best to have a round of the game while Aunt Gioia was occupied with looking at dresses or choosing groceries in the food hall. Taking it in turns to be the hider or the seeker, we would go to the very top of the store to begin, the idea being that the hider had to get all the way to the bottom of the building, which had seven floors, including the basement, without being spotted by the seeker.

Jill and I must have driven the store's staff and customers crazy as we shrieked, laughed and hollered our way through every department, disguising ourselves in racks of ball gowns and fur coats or popping out from behind displays. We were so noisy and excited as we played. Fortunately, possibly because Aunt Gioia was such a good Harrods customer, we weren't ever asked to leave.

CHAPTER ELEVEN

Jean

Unlike the house in Kinnerton Street, Newland Hall was perpetually cold. When Uncle Tom, Aunt Gioia and Jill, came to stay with us, Aunt Gioia would always commandeer the airing cupboard as her writing space, claiming that it was the only place in the house warm enough for her to be able to think. Having grown up in Italy, Aunt Gioia was used to much hotter and drier weather and very much disliked the damp Lancashire air. She once said that if Newland Hall were ever to catch fire, she would throw all the logs onto it because they were so damp they would soon put the flames out.

While Aunt Gioia was scribbling away in the airing cupboard, like a character straight out of a Nancy Mitford novel, the rest of us kept warm by sitting right by a fireplace or staying tucked up in bed. There were no fires in the bedrooms. Grandboffin had actually had central heating of a sort fitted at Newland. The problem was that for some reason the central heating pipes had been laid so that after they left the coke-fired boiler, they went through the boot room and out into the yard before coming back into the house again, which meant that any hot water had already cooled down long before it got as far as any bathroom or bedroom radiator. Added to that, the house was large and rambling so that some corners never had hot water at all. Hence poor Ellen having to carry water up to all the bedrooms every morning.

Grandboffin had also fitted the house with electricity. A little shed on the way up to the estate farm housed the new-fangled generator. Unfortunately, like the central heating, Grandboffin's experiment with electricity wasn't a terrific success. When the generator was running at full pelt, we had wonderfully bright light but the whole house shook because the generator was so loud; but if the generator wasn't running fast enough to shake the house, the lights were dim and flickered too much to be of any use. It wasn't much of a choice!

It was partly because Newland Hall was so very cold in the winter that a visit to the Cliff Mill, our family's cotton mill in Preston, always felt like such a treat.

Our family had been in farming for generations but in the 19th century, our great-grandfather Henry Owtram started working in the textile industry, travelling to France to buy fabric. Fascinated by what he saw in the French mills, he went into manufacturing. His son Herbert Hawkesworth, our grandfather – Grandboffin – followed in Henry's footsteps and spent his whole life in the industry, eventually becoming a director of Horrockses, one of Lancashire's biggest textile companies. It was Grandboffin who bought the Cliff Mill.

The textile industry shaped not only the history of our family but the history of the whole of the north-west of

England. In the 1920s Lancashire was the centre of cotton spinning and weaving in Britain, with many towns around the country specialising in the manufacture of different cotton products.

Because cotton needs warm temperatures to grow, Lancashire was obviously not somewhere cotton plants could ever thrive but the county did have several natural advantages that made it an ideal manufacturing hub. Firstly, it was blessed with resources that enabled the cheap running of mills. There were plenty of streams to drive the water mills and coal to power the steam engines that came later. The year-round damp climate of Lancashire was also advantageous, making it less likely that the fragile cotton fibres would snap during the spinning process. Last but not least, by the time the industrial revolution arrived, the county already had a highly-skilled workforce, thanks to a long tradition of spinning and weaving in the area. The mechanisation of the cotton industry had an enormous impact on Lancashire's economy. At the end of the 19th century, one in every eight Lancastrians was employed in the textile business.

In the 1920s, there were 60 mills in Preston alone but by the time Pat and I were old enough to visit Cliff Mill with our father, the industry was already somewhat in decline. The development of mills in former markets for British cotton – such as India and Japan – saw those countries becoming manufacturers and exporters in their own right. Meanwhile the United States had introduced punitive tariffs on British goods, making the previously lucrative cross-Atlantic trade all but impossible.

Despite the changes that were underway, the Cliff Mill still felt very busy when we visited as children. The mill was a huge brick building with a tall chimney, built in 1904 (it was actually the last to be built in Preston), that towered over the neat terraced streets that had sprung up around it. Within its boundaries was a stable where donkeys used to transport goods around the mill once lived.

Inside, the building throbbed with the sound of the two enormous engines that powered the spinning machines. The engines were so important that they had names. They were called 'Patience' and 'Rotha', after Patience and Rotha Hollins, daughters of the family who owned the mill before our family took over. The engines were christened in a ceremony, attended by local dignitaries and reported in the press, where Miss Rotha Hollins performed the traditional ritual of turning the engines on and off for the first time and Grandboffin gave a vote of thanks.

Everything in the mill vibrated in time to those engines. The noise was tremendous. Once you were inside the mill, it was very hard to hear what anyone said but the people who worked there were able to understand one another perfectly, without raising their voices, having developed the ability to lip-read. I found that fascinating and tried hard to do the same myself.

Cliff Mill was what was known as a 'spinning mill', turning raw cotton into thread that would then be sent on to a weaving mill. Other mills, such as Horrockses, were 'vertical' mills, which took the cotton through the whole process from raw bale to finished fabric. The cotton itself was grown in Egypt and Sudan and transported by boat to Liverpool. On Fridays, our father and Grandboffin were always 'on change', which meant that they had gone to the cotton exchange in Liverpool or Manchester to swap information about cotton prices and quality with their fellow mill owners.

At Christmas, the cotton brokers with whom our father traded always sent generous presents. Among our favourites were the gifts from a friendly Greek trader who sent such delicacies as rose petals in syrup, Turkish delight and pistachio nuts. Luxuries indeed for children raised on the blandest of nursery puddings!

The raw cotton arrived in huge soft white fluffy bales that looked as though they might be fun to climb into. I certainly thought so. Then I heard that one bale, when it was opened, was found to contain the squashed corpse of an unfortunate Egyptian worker who must have fallen into the cotton as it was being bundled up. I don't know whether that was a true story but it certainly made me look at the bales differently from then on.

Whenever Pat and I visited Cliff Mill, the people who worked there were always very kind to us. The mill was a close community and, while we were there, we were made to feel like part of the team. But times were changing.

Our family sold the Cliff Mill in the 1960s. After a brief resurgence during the Second World War, when the Lancashire mills shifted to making cotton for military uniforms, the textile industry in the UK went into a terminal decline. The imposing red-brick building that used to throb to the twin heartbeats of Patience and Rotha was turned into a supermarket in the 1970s; first called Gem, then Fame, and then Asda. But the supermarket did not last either. The mill was finally demolished in the late 1980s and houses were built on the site.

Mill work was very hard and sometimes dangerous and I doubt that many people would sign up to work in Cliff Mill today but it's sad to think that the building which seemed so solid and eternal to Pat and I as children did not make it to her 100th birthday.

CHAPTER TWELVE

Pat

In many ways, our Lancashire childhood was idyllic, but as Virgil's ancient poem reminds us: 'Et in Arcadia ego'. The most dramatic event of our childhood was undoubtedly 'The Murder', which brought the spectre of death into our young lives on the most ordinary of days.

It happened on a Sunday morning in the spring of 1931, when Jean and I were respectively seven and five years old. Sundays always began with a visit to St Mark's in Dolphinholme and on this particular day I was especially excited to be going to church, having been given 2d to put in the collection box rather than the customary 1d. It felt like an important promotion. Our mother loaded us into the car as usual and we were almost at the village when we happened upon a small group of people gathered at the side of the road. There was much shouting and panic.

'Don't look out of the windows,' our mother exclaimed, as she suddenly braked and pulled our car over to the verge. 'Pat! Jean! Don't look out!'

It was already too late.

While our mother scrambled to pull down the blinds over the passenger windows so that we might not see what was going on, Jean and I did our best to see around her. A motorcycle lay on the tarmac; its still-turning wheels suggesting it had only recently been abandoned. A little further on lay two bodies in what appeared to be pools of sticky dark blood.

Our first thought was that there must have been an accident. While our mother continued her desperate attempts to shield us from the horrible scene, Jean and I tried hard to commit it to memory, imagining how we'd share the excitement of it all with our friends at Sunday School. It was the most extraordinary thing we'd ever witnessed.

Defeated by the blinds – or rather by our determined efforts to see around them – our mother got out of the car to see if there was any way she could assist.

Alas, there was nothing to be done for the two poor people on the road. A young man and woman, they were both beyond any help. The woman was already dead and the man was moments from dying. White-faced but saying nothing about the truth of the situation, our mother climbed back into the driver's seat. She drove quickly on towards the church, where the puzzled vicar paced the empty nave, wondering what had become of his congregation.

Jean and I were thrilled to have caught a glimpse of the drama unfolding, as small children often are thrilled by the things that rightly horrify their elders.

That incident on the road to Dolphinholme was the most exciting thing we had ever seen; but the truth of the matter was desperately tragic.

A few years later at boarding school, when I started thinking that I might pursue a career as a journalist, I wrote an account of the inquest in true newspaper style.

MURDER SHOT SCARES VILLAGE CHURCHGOERS. THWARTED LOVER SHOOTS SELF AND GIRL.

A Montagu-Capulet drama of two thwarted lovers, culminating last Sunday in a double tragedy, shocked the people of Carnstead, peaceful little North Lancashire village.

Interesting evidence at an inquest in Lancaster today on WALTER PYE, 23-year-old railway porter, of Fell End Farm, Carnstead, and MINNIE GRIFFITHS, 21 years old, of Greenbank Millhouse, Carnstead, revealed a tragic story of lovers prevented from marrying by a family feud.

Flour miller Albert Griffiths, father of three daughters, of which Minnie was the eldest, has long had no dealings with farmer George Pye, whose second son Walter worked as a porter at the local station. The trouble originally arose over a boundary dispute in 1925, followed in 1929 by a charge of theft, in connection with some professional work done by Mr Griffiths for Mr Pye, which was brought against him by Mr Pye, who lost the case. In 1936 Mr Griffiths' hayricks were fired, and he brought a case against Mr Pye, but this was squashed as there was insufficient proof.

Late December, Walter Pye and Minnie Griffiths met at a local dance and fell in love. Their parents forbade the match, and Mrs Griffiths stated in evidence that her daughter seemed to have abandoned all idea of continuing the project, though she was naturally upset about it at first.

Several local witnesses testified to the curious behaviour of Walter Pye at this time. They had seen him on several occasions walking beside the Canal in the early hours of the morning, and the Stationmaster stated that he himself had once intervened to prevent Pye throwing himself under an express train. Mr George Pye said,

'We noticed ourselves that there was something wrong with Walter, but thought it best to leave him to himself.'

17-year-old farm hand Tom Winder, in the employ of Mr Sam Cookson, outside whose farm the fatality occurred, stated that at 10.20 am on the morning of Sunday, November 17th, he was leaning on a field-gate on the opposite side of the road to Mr Cookson's farm, watching the churchgoers pass.

WINDER. I saw Mrs Griffiths coming along with Minnie and Elsie. Minnie was in the middle. They were all talking and going slow because it was still early on. Then I heard a motorbike a long way behind them. I thought it might have been a pal of mine, so I waited to see, but when he came over the top of the hill, I saw it was Walter Pye. I was surprised, because I'd never seen him going to church before. He slowed down and parked his bike at the side of the road, near where I was. I said, "Hullo, Walter," but he never answered. He was looking very white and grim. He walked after Mrs Griffiths and Minnie and Elsie, quiet but rapid and purposeful. I thought I'd better get back to carting muck, which was what I'd been doing before.

Winder then went on to state that about three minutes later he heard two shots, and ran up the road to the farm, where several people were already gathering.

Mrs Griffiths, who was in mourning and seemed deeply afflicted, stated that she and her daughters were just opposite Brade Hill Farm when they heard quick steps following them.

As she turned, Pye put his right arm round Minnie from behind her, and shot her through the heart with a revolver. Mrs Griffiths broke down as she described how Minnie had gasped – "Mother!" and fallen backwards.

Elsie Griffiths, 19-year-old sister of Minnie Griffiths, then continued the evidence.

"He kissed her passionately on the mouth," she stated. "Then he raised the revolver to his right ear and shot himself through the head. It was horrible."

Mr. Sam Cookson then gave evidence. He had been in the kitchen when he heard the first shot, which was followed by screams from Mrs Griffiths and Elsie.

COOKSON. Then came another shot and I laid hold of my rook rifle and ran out.

CORONER. Were you afraid?

COOKSON. No. I'm an old soldier.

CORONER. You are a brave man, Mr Cookson.

COOKSON. Thank you, sir. When I got on to the road, I saw Elsie supporting Mrs Griffiths, who looked to be in a bad way. I told Elsie to take her into our kitchen, which she did. Minnie was lying on her back on the road: she was dead all right. Young Pye was about a yard from her with his head in a pool of blood that was splashed all over the road. He was still moving a bit.

CORONER. Did you make any attempt to save his life?

COOKSON. No, I knew he would only have hung if I had so I left him. But our Tom came running up, and I sent him off on his bicycle for the doctor. Pye died about two minutes after I first came out.

Cookson was then allowed to stand down, and the vicar (Rev. Learoyd Marsh), Dr Stones, and Police Sergeant John Matthews gave evidence.

Dr Stones affirmed that death in the case of Minnie Griffiths was due to internal haemorrhage caused by a gun-shot through the dorsal aorta, resulting in instantaneous death; and in the case of Pye, violent fracture of the skull caused practically instantaneous death.

The inquest was adjourned till Monday, when further evidence will be given, probably of a sensational nature and our reporter will be on the spot as usual.

My account of the murder-suicide is full of detail but none of it was quite accurate. Unable to recall the exact details, having been so young at the time of the incident, I'd made up the names and the dates, mixing the real with the fictional.

Researching the truth of the episode many years later, I learned that the real victim was 18-year-old Belle Porter, of Marsden Hall Farm. Her killer, 21-year-old John William Hurst, was a plumber and promising amateur football player from Goosnargh.

The real inquest, reported in the local papers of the time, revealed a tragedy that had been brewing for quite some while. Belle and John had fallen in love but their families raised objections to the match because of a difference of religion. The Porter family were Nonconformist and attended the Independent Methodist Chapel. The Hurst family were Roman Catholic. Jack Porter forbade his daughter Belle from seeing John. It was then that John's quest for vengeance began. He twice set fire to the Porter family barn.

On the morning of the murder, knowing that Belle and her family would be going to church, Hurst got on his motorbike and headed out to intercept them. He caught up with the Porter children on the road into the village and shot Belle in the head. After he killed Belle, Hurst did not kill himself right away but instead taunted Belle's father Jack Porter as they stood face-to-face over her body, showing him a small jar of phosphorus and saying, 'Look, Jack. This is what has burnt your barn down.' It was only then that Hurst turned his back to Porter, put the gun in his own mouth and took his own life; 'falling like a tree' in the words of one witness. He did not die right away.

One aspect of my account that remained true to the facts was the evidence of Mr Sam Cookson. Jean remembers seeing Cookson that long ago morning and her own account of Cookson's plain Lancashire words to our mother, has added poignancy. Jean wrote, 'Our mother, having found that poor, heart-broken Hurst was still alive, urged someone to fetch a doctor, but Cookson responded with blinding practical logic, "Why worry? 'e'll nobbut 'ang." Which was unarguable.'

Sam Cookson was right. The death penalty was still very much in place in the 1930s.

When I was in my early teens, I secretly followed what would become one of Lancashire's most notorious criminal cases, known as 'The Jigsaw Murders'. My parents tried to shield me from the story, preventing me from reading reports about the case in the papers, but I picked up the gossip all the same. The 1935 case involved the gruesome discovery of dismembered human remains by walkers in the Scottish Borders. While the killer had tried to disguise his victims' identities by removing identifying parts such as fingertips, he had foolishly wrapped some of the evidence that remained in sheets torn from the *Sunday Graphic*, Morecambe and Lancaster edition.

Suspicion soon fell on Lancaster GP Dr Buck Ruxton, whose wife Isabella and children's nanny, Mary Rogerson, had recently disappeared. Dr Ruxton claimed they'd gone together to visit Isabella's family in Scotland. Ruxton was an unlikely suspect, well-liked by his patients – he was known to have waived his fees for patients who couldn't afford his services – but the missing women and the Lancashire connection of the newspaper were too big a coincidence to ignore.

The police forces of Dumfriesshire and Lancaster worked together to identify the bodies found in the Borders using groundbreaking new forensic techniques. Photographs of the skulls were superimposed onto family photographs of the two missing women. They made a perfect match. Casts of the victims' feet fitted neatly into the missing women's shoes. A single fingerprint, identifying one of the arms found as belonging to Mary Rogerson sealed Ruxton's fate. He was found guilty of murder and thousands of onlookers queued to see him be hanged at Manchester's Strangeways jail. He protested his innocence to the very end.

I had no sympathy for Dr Ruxton, but all these years later, the tragic story of Belle Porter and John Hurst still haunts me. However, that same year another forbidden love story was unfolding that had the whole nation transfixed.

CHAPTER THIRTEEN

Pat

Jean and I were raised to be royalists and had very conventional thoughts about what the monarchy was supposed to represent. When George V and Queen Mary travelled to nearby Abbeystead House, where they stayed as guests of the Earl of Sefton, we turned out to wave flags as the royal car passed through Dolphinholme. I remember seeing Queen Mary wave back at us in a manner that suggested she was rather bored of her loyal subjects. Our mother captured the moment in a blurry photograph of the royal car. You can just about see that Queen Mary is wearing her traditional toque, the brimless style of hat she made popular, as she sits bolt upright in the back seat.

On May 6th, 1935, George V and Queen Mary celebrated 25 years on the throne and the nation celebrated with them. Fiery beacons were lit up and down the country.

Our family attended a special thanksgiving service at church in Dolphinholme. After the service, there was a celebratory parade and an afternoon of sports. We children were each given a commemorative mug and a set of jubilee stamps to mark the occasion. It was a joyful day.

Alas, less than a year later, George V, who had long-suffered from a chronic lung issue, was taken ill and died. Confined to bed by measles at the time, I wrote about the King's death in my diary.

At 11.55pm, on January 20th, 1936, King George died peacefully at Sandringham, in the presence of the Royal Family. I was having measles. Little Denis Singleton died a little after and Rudyard Kipling just before the king (at about 9pm the BBC sent out the most tragic message it ever had, the last bulletin but one: it said 'The King's life is passing peacefully towards its close').
'On January 28th, King George was buried in St George's Chapel, Windsor. Daddy went up for the funeral. We listened in to the procession round London. The pipes played "Over the sea to Skye" beautifully. It was so suitable, "the lad that was born to be King".

Immediately after his death, the Palace sent out the news that in his final hours the King had convened a meeting of his privy council and that he used his last breath to enquire about the state of the Empire. A few days later a rumour began to circulate that the King's last words, given in response to a suggestion that he might like to recuperate from this latest bout of ill health in Bognor Regis, were actually 'Bugger Bognor'. The King's physician, however, wrote in his diary that George V's last words were in fact 'God damn you'.

Whatever his parting shot, the loss of George V was very sad indeed but I was quietly delighted at the thought of his handsome eldest son becoming King Edward VIII. At the beginning of my 1937 diary, I compiled a list of 'heroes', not unlike a list of television and pop stars a modern teenager might compile today. I added the names of a few 'Ghastlys' too. I wrote:

> *I have heroes inside me nearly as much as Jean, but secretly. Nobody knows about them, except that I admire King Edward VIII. No-one else seems to like him a bit. This is my list of heroes – not so long as Jean's.*
> *VVM His Majesty King Edward VIII (very very much)*
> *VM His Majesty King Leopold of Belgium (very much)*
> *Q His Highness the Prince of Piedmont (quite)*
> *VM His Highness Prince Charles Edward Stuart (very much)*
> *VVM Lawrence of Arabia (very much)*
> *Q Drake (quite)*
> *Q Laurence Olivier (quite)*
> *VM His Highness the Duke of Kent (very)*
> *GHASTLYS – Hitler, Caballero, Mussolini, the Ex-Kaiser, and Charlotte M. Yonge's heroes, are my pet abominations.*

I don't know why I had such antipathy for the heroes of Christian writer Charlotte M Yonge, author of the 'Heir of Redclyffe', but I was a fan of Edward VIII from the very beginning. So you can imagine how keen I was to see that our new bachelor king found a worthy queen. Secretly, I suppose I hoped it might even be me. When the news broke that he was in love with Mrs Wallis Simpson, I was devastated. But I wasn't the only one who felt let down.

Edward VIII's love for Wallis Simpson scandalised the

nation. Tradition dictated that the king should marry a certain type of woman and Wallis Simpson was not the virginal young princess everyone expected a royal bride to be. Far from it. Mrs Simpson was an American socialite from Baltimore, who had been married not once but twice before. Her first marriage, in 1916, was to a United States Navy officer called Earl Winfield Spencer Junior, known as Win (Earl was his Christian name rather than his title). They divorced in 1927. It was during her second marriage, to Ernest Simpson, an American-born British shipbroker, that Mrs Simpson met Edward VIII, who was then the Prince of Wales, and set her sights on marrying a real aristocrat. Shortly after Edward VIII's accession to the throne, Mrs Simpson divorced her second husband with the intention of becoming Edward's queen.

Not only did the King's love for an American divorcee with two living ex-husbands break my heart, it caused a constitutional crisis. There was no precedent for such a departure from tradition. The King could not possibly marry a twice-divorced woman. He was the head of the Church of England and thus must surely be held to a higher moral standard than the rest of us.

The adults tried to shield us children from the news, but – as with 'The Jigsaw Murder' case – I read every newspaper article I could lay my hands on and kept my ears open for grown-up gossip. Naturally, I wrote in my diary about the unfolding drama, which took place against the backdrop of tragedy at home, with the death of Jean's beloved puppy Sam and then, to everyone's horror, the sudden death a couple of days later of Murphy the gardener in a road accident not far from Newland. Further afield, Spain descended into civil war. Those newspaper columns that weren't taken up with opinions on Edward VIII and Mrs Simpson, described the horror unfolding on the Iberian Peninsula in sometimes graphic detail.

My diary entries from the time reveal how, as a young teenager, I tried to make sense of it all, jumbling together the personal, the national and the international events – the everyday, the banal and the deeply shocking – as they happened. War and death are recorded in the same breath as new kittens, cinema visits and Christmas shopping.

Dec 3rd: A lot has happened today, which is a Thursday. This morning we did lessons and went for a long walk, taking Sam, who is a spaniel puppy and belongs to Jean. This afternoon, Mummy and I went to Lancaster. We saw Dr Kay, who says I am to have sun-ray treatment at the infirmary. There is an awful fuss going on about the King and Mrs Simpson. It is so surprising, as he has been a perfect King up till now. I expect it is only the beastly Americans. The King is staying at Fort Belvedere. This afternoon, Sam died, Murphy had him out and he just died. They have not told Jean: and they are still besieging Madrid.

Dec 4th: Today is fine and rather cold. The affair about the King is getting worse. He is determined to marry her, refuses to compromise, and is talking of abdicating. Mummy told Jean about Sam this morning. They are still besieging Madrid, and we went for a walk with the Welches. I had my hair washed yesterday, and it will be untidy today. Ellen went this afternoon, and there are four kittens.

Dec 5th: Saturday. There was a shoot here today. At 10.20 this morning the local Guide Commissioners came round, collecting our parcels for the poor children. At 11.30 I had sun-ray treatment in the infirmary. In the afternoon we went to a party at Mary Storey's. It was rather fun. Mummy and Mrs Sterpaker are doing the cooking, we are hoping a temporary will come on Tuesday. Tonight Murphy was bicycling through Galgate when Ted Brown ran into him, and Murphy died two hours later, in the infirmary, sometime after 11. Not much news about the King.

Dec 6th: We went to church this morning. This afternoon we had children's service and a rehearsal for our Nativity Play in the church. It is bitterly cold and the hills are covered with snow. The King will either have to abdicate or give up Mrs Simpson. Because the Cabinet refuse to make a new law to prevent her being Queen. The inquest on Murphy is going to be held on Thursday.

Dec 7th: Monday. This afternoon we did some of our Christmas shopping in Marks and Spencer's. I bought 12 1/2d cards (6d), a book for Jean (1s) a box of King Edward chocolates for Mummy and Daddy, because there was such a nice picture of him on the lid (1/6) and two tins of toffees for Paddy and Jill (6d each). Murphy's inquest was held today. The King and Madrid remained in the same position.

Dec 8th: Tuesday. Had sun-ray treatment in the morning, and saw Dr Kay and Dr Stewart, we went on a walk this morning. Very cold but fine. Did lessons all the afternoon. The new Scottish cook, Miss Hollins, arrived this afternoon. She is old and a little fearsome.

Dec 9th: Wednesday. When I am writing this, Daddy and Mummy and Grandboffin have gone to Murphy's funeral. Jean, Bobby and I sent a little wreath. Mrs Simpson is willing to back out of the whole affair if it will clear up the muddle. We are going to walk round and have tea with the Woods this afternoon. It is bitterly cold and frost, but sunny today... We went to tea with the Woods. It was rather fun. There is another awful fog tonight. The Welches had a smash tonight but they are all still well and alive.

Dec 10th: A lot happened today. This morning it was very foggy and cold. I had sun-ray treatment and did lessons. This afternoon it was clearer, and Mummy took Miss Allen and Joy and us to see 'Little Lord Fauntleroy' at the Odeon. Freddie Bartholomew and the old Earl were very good, but I did not like Dearest much. Daddy had a cold and stayed in bed all day. Everybody was very worried about the King. When we got back at four o'clock this afternoon we heard that he had abdicated. I am awfully sorry he did. I hope the Duke of York will be a good king but he can't be so nice. King Edward is leaving England tomorrow night to join Mrs Simpson in France. This evening we listened in. The announcer said the King's speech and Mr Baldwin's account of the whole affair. It actually began in August when people got a bit worried about the American newspapers, which were suggesting things. Mr Baldwin went to the King and had a talk with him. King Edward sent for him again on November 16th and told him he was going to marry Mrs Simpson. On November 25th, King Edward again sent for him and asked him whether they would pass a law making Mrs Simpson not queen? Mr Baldwin had already made research into this matter and replied, No. Ever since that time the King has been making up his mind. I loathe Americans!

Dec 11th: Friday. The new King is going to be called George VI instead of Albert I, for which I am glad. The Bill of Abdication passed through both houses and was agreed to by King George VI today. It took 2hrs, 37 minutes. Now King Edward is an ordinary subject of King George but I shall always think of him as the King.

CHAPTER FOURTEEN

Pat

Despite the best efforts of the establishment to persuade him otherwise, Edward VIII chose love over duty. That Christmas, Uncle Godfrey joked about the whole affair, singing to the tune of 'Hark the Herald Angels' – 'Hark the herald angels sing, Mrs Simpson stole our king.' I did not find it as funny as I might have done. I was very disappointed in our erstwhile king, believing as I did that he should have controlled his romantic urges and put duty first. Perhaps it's old fashioned to say so, but I still feel that being king is not a role one should cast off lightly.

A new royal family was waiting in the wings but in January 1937, I was still very upset about the whole affair. I couldn't see how Edward's shy younger brother, who had none of Edward's charisma and who struggled with a stammer that made public speaking difficult, could possibly step into the role. I wrote in my diary:

When King Edward went it left a sort of hole in me somewhere, and the new king does not fill it up. I can't work up the least interest in George VIth. It all went to Edward. When I first heard, last spring, that the Welches were going to the Coronation, I was consumed with envy.

*But now it is not King Edward who is being crowned, I
don't care a bit. I expect all this is treason so I had better
say no more. But it is awful to think that King Edward has
gone for ever and ever.*

I think perhaps I took Edward VIII's abdication especially
badly for reasons other than pure outrage at his romantic
choices. Murphy's death was unsettling. We'd known him
for practically all our lives and the manner of his death –
knocked off his bicycle by a car on a blind corner – was so
awful and sudden.

I had also been suffering from ill health. The 'sun-ray
treatment' was for a problem with my neck, perhaps related
to the bovine tuberculosis I must have contracted from the
unpasteurised milk we drank at Newland Hall. I would suffer
from recurrences of the infection throughout my teens and
early twenties.

The treatment, sun-ray therapy, was very popular in the
'30s and '40s. Patients were prescribed sessions under ultra-
violet light for all sorts of conditions including sore throats,
tonsillitis and skin ailments such as acne and psoriasis. Unfortunately, sun-ray treatment did not work for me at all, and I
had to have an operation to remove a lump on my neck. It
was very frustrating, though I did enjoy being sent to recuperate in Torquay.

On top of that, one of my dearest personal ambitions had
recently been thwarted. In November of 1936, my Aunt
Gioia, who had been doing her very best to find a publisher
for my first novel, wrote with bad news.

Enclosed is Pat's little book. I am afraid it got a bit knocked about at the last agents to whom I sent it. They returned it earlier this week. Jolly typed out for me the agent's comments, which I send herewith. I am so sorry I couldn't get it off. I believed strongly in it myself, but people don't have the sense to jump to something fresh and new if the idea isn't exactly like everything they've ever seen before. Most people don't, anyway.

The publishing world wasn't ready for me.

Finally, just as seems to be the case today whenever one turns on the television, the news coming out of the wider world was most unnerving. The siege of Madrid, which I mentioned in my diary, began in October 1936. The siege, which would last for two and a half years, was one of the key battles in the Spanish Civil War. The conflict had been brought vividly to my attention by a photograph, published in the *Daily Mail*, of a young man – a republican – about to be executed by members of the Nationalist Army. So many years later, I can still see that photograph quite clearly in my mind's eye. It shocked me to the core, to see this young man, not so much older than I was, captured on film in the last moments of his life and I wanted to know how on earth such an atrocious situation came about.

I read as much as I could about the civil war, which arose out of the polarisation of Spanish society into nationalist and republican groups. The nationalists broadly comprised the country's establishment: the military, the landowners, the wealthy. The republicans comprised the working and middle classes. The civil war began with a failed military coup by The nationalists against Spain's Republican government. The nationalists were backed by conservatives within Spain but they also received support from Fascist Italy and Nazi Germany. Meanwhile, the republicans were aided by the Soviet Union and joined in their fight by volunteers from all over Europe and the United States, who came together in 'International Brigades'.

The thought of civil war was very frightening and the business with Edward VIII and Wallis Simpson had brought home the fact that even the British monarchy, which seemed to me to be the very cornerstone of our society, was not the unshakeable institution I had always assumed it to be. The abdication had shown me that at any moment all our certainties might be upended.

Less than a month after Edward VIII stepped down, our beloved maternal grandmother Gaggie died after a long illness. She was buried in Bath and right afterwards, our maternal grandfather, Pops, came to stay with us at Newland Hall. It was a difficult start to the new year.

But while I was very reluctant to accept the abdication in January '37, I eventually came around to the idea of our new king, George VI (ultimately, I forgave the beastly Americans too, when I worked alongside them during the War and later studied at Harvard). Jean and I were both fascinated by the young Princesses Elizabeth and Margaret, so close to us in age, who had suddenly been catapulted right to the top of the line of succession. Seeing photographs of the young princesses with their pet dogs in the newspaper, we were happy to think we had a great deal in common with our future queen and her little sister. Yes, we were very pleased at the idea of a royal family that seemed so similar to our own, but how daunting it must have been for the young girl who would one day become Elizabeth II, to have to shoulder that impossibly heavy weight of national expectation and duty at such a tender age.

CHAPTER FIFTEEN

Jean

As the years passed, both Pat and I were very glad that Edward VIII made way for his brother George VI, who was quite a different sort of character. Though it's been said that Queen Elizabeth the Queen Mother never forgave her brother-in-law for forcing her shy, stammering husband onto the throne, George VI made a very good king and turned out to be exactly the right man to lead the nation through the Second World War. Likewise, in her turn, his daughter made an excellent queen.

Pat and I watched the progress of Elizabeth II with great interest and affection. Were it not for the *coup de foudre* of Edward VII and Wallis Simpson that altered the trajectory of her young life so dramatically, the young princess might have led a life not so very different to ours. Instead, she took on the mantle of a Queen and set her personal freedom to one side to serve the nation. And how diligently and well she fulfilled her role.

Having lived our lives in a sort of lockstep with the Queen, we were very sad indeed to hear the news of her death in September 2022. I shall always remember the afternoon in 1951 when Pat and I had occasion to meet Her Majesty and her sister Princess Margaret when we were presented at court.

Our Aunt Marjorie, my godmother, was very keen on 'society'. Throughout the war she had done her best to keep up with her social obligations by organising tea dances at the Grosvenor Hotel for visiting servicemen. Aunt Marjorie was determined that Pat and I should not miss out on being presented to the King and Queen, as was expected of girls of our class, just because there had been a war. She arranged for Pat, me and our mother to be invited to what was known as a 'drawing room' – a tea-time reception at Buckingham Palace. Apparently, tradition dictated that our mother had to be presented first, before Pat and I were deemed fit to be seen by the King.

Pat and I were both very busy young women by this time. Having spent a couple of years in Norway, helping to reinstate the British embassy there, Pat was studying for a degree in literature at St Andrews. Meanwhile, I had been working all over Europe for a variety of refugee missions, before returning to the UK to train as a social worker. Pat was as cross as two sticks to receive the invitation – or rather the summons – to the palace, as it came right before her final university exams. All the same, we did not want to upset Aunt Marjorie and so we said we'd be delighted to meet her in London. It would give us a chance to see the Festival of Britain too.

There was, of course, a formal dress code for the palace. Neither Pat nor I had extensive wardrobes full of suitable clothes for such fancy occasions and Pat was forced to buy something new. She chose a mauve dress decorated with sequins for ten guineas. She didn't dare tell our mother how much it had cost. Aunt Marjorie lent our mother a fur coat for the day. I was just glad that one could wear a short dress and didn't have to bother with all the debutante frills and feathers.

Arriving at the Palace, we were ushered into a waiting room. Being nosey, as we were led down a corridor, I peeked into a room where a rather threadbare-looking throne stood abandoned in the centre of the floor. Eventually, we were led into the room where King George VI and his Queen awaited us. There we joined a line of other men and women waiting to bow and curtsey in front of the monarch. The etiquette was very strict and we were informed that once the King had finished talking to us, we were to leave the room without turning our backs on him. It was quite the performance!

I remember thinking that the King did not look well that day. Underneath a surprising amount of panstick, his skin was yellowish and clammy and I was worried for his health. The very last thing he needed was to have to spend the afternoon pretending to be interested in strangers. I wanted to say to him, 'For goodness' sake. Just get up and go and have a rest.' His wife, the Queen (later the Queen Mother), also seemed concerned as she glanced across at him.

Afterwards, we were taken into another room for tea. The Princesses Elizabeth and Margaret were there too, but for the most part, they remained in a corner talking only to one another, which seemed a shame, since we might have found we had a great deal in common. Princess Elizabeth had been in the ATS (Auxiliary Territorial Service) during the war and I imagine some of her experiences might have been similar to those I had had in the First Aid Nursing Yeomanry. Instead, Pat and I chatted with each other and I made friends with a palace cat, a rather scruffy animal who nevertheless walked through the gilded rooms with as much confidence as any high-born prince.

Later, we were glad we had 'been done'. It was especially useful for me to have been presented at court, since it meant that, when I was working overseas, I was able to present myself at the British Embassy wherever I arrived and would then be invited to embassy parties. On the day itself, the whole event seemed slightly ridiculous, with all the arcane ceremony and ritual, but by far the funniest moment was when Pat and I sat down to tea and discovered that while her silver teaspoon bore the royal crest, mine – silver-plated – bore the trademark of Lyons, the tea-houses, who must have been responsible for the catering!

CHAPTER SIXTEEN

Pat

Back in the spring of 1937, the nation began to plan for the coronation of a new king. While George VI may not have been the king we were expecting to crown that year, there would of course still be great celebrations.

Though I had claimed that I didn't envy our friends the Welches, who were heading to London for the main event, as Coronation day drew closer, I started to change my mind, writing, 'Now I feel a little bit envious of the Welches going to the Coronation – in fact, quite a large bit. They will see King Leopold (who I secretly admire) and Piedmont, and heaps of exciting people. They are lucky.'

When the day came, I contented myself with celebrating in Dolphinholme, recording events for posterity in my diary.

May 12th. Coronation day at last! Everywhere decorated. We went to the service in Dolphinholme church and I prayed for the King like mad. Afterwards we got our mugs and rushed back to listen in. We heard nearly the whole service, and I did so want to howl throughout. It was so historic and wonderful, and felt so never-can-happen-again-ish. The fanfares were just beautiful, and I like the King's voice awfully, though he does have to speak slow to stop his stammer. We went to the sports in the afternoon. I think our King will be the best ever. I think he will be better than even Edward. We heard him broadcast in the evening. I thought that he was going to break down at first, because there was a pause and gulpy noises before he began, but he did it 'somethink looverly'. It makes it more impressive, him talking so slow.

There were splendid pictures and accounts and special supplements in the papers the next day. I don't like the new coins much: the 3d bits are octangular and very thick and heavy. I have two. The pennies have a lighthouse on them, which is nice, and the florins and 1-s are different and the shillings Scots are quite different to the shillings English. The 1/4ds have a wren on them, which is charming, and the half-pennies a ship.'

We had a new king and my life was changing too. At the end of that particular diary entry, I wrote, 'Daddy and Mummy were going to look at schools for me on Saturday and they decided to take me too.'

Jean and I both learned to read at an early age and for a very long time I had been desperate to go to school. There was a small village school in Dolphinholme but our parents decided that they would prefer for us to be educated at home, by governesses, just as our mother had been.

In fact, to begin my education, my parents employed the services of Miss Harrison, who had been governess to my mother. More than 20 years had passed since then, so I suppose my parents shouldn't have been too surprised that

Miss Harrison's teaching methods were a little out of date. Miss Harrison was very much more effective as a teacher of English and history than of maths or Latin. Fortunately, I was very happy to spend most of my time working on Miss Harrison's pet subjects. I could think of nothing better than being allowed to read novels or history books all day long.

One of Miss Harrison's favourite things was to set me little dictations. I found that I was rather good at these and soon I was getting a mark of 100 per cent every time. Seeing that I was doing so well, Miss Harrison mused, 'Perhaps I should make the dictations more difficult.'

'Not on any account!' was my instant reply.

But I had to advance and ultimately that meant moving ahead with another teacher. After Miss Harrison came Miss Clayton. Enid Clayton hailed from Kendal and had been trained as a teacher by the PNEU: the Parents National Educational Union, an organisation formed in Bradford in the 1880s, which provided resources for home-schooling based on the teachings of Charlotte Mason.

Mason was an educational pioneer, born in Wales in the 1840s. Inspired by the bible, she believed that all children have a natural love for learning and that teaching should always be 'child-centred'. She believed in the importance of reading literature that sparked the imagination, rather than filling children's heads with useless facts. Her methods certainly suited me. But being taught at home by a governess could be an isolating experience, so during the summer the PNEU organised large get-togethers in the Lake District, where homeschooled children from all over the north-west could meet their peers and make new friends. It's perhaps no coincidence that Mason is credited with inspiring the early scouting movement too.

Our PNEU-trained governess, Miss Clayton, was very efficient, serious and methodical. She was a vicar's daughter and as such she was very keen on bible readings and 'good behaviour'. She was also a keen nature lover and would often take us on walks in the local countryside. She taught us the names of all the plants in the garden – in English and in Latin – and came with us to gather blackberries in the autumn.

We loved Miss Clayton so much that we were very happy to stay with her while our parents took a little holiday in Scotland. Just as Nanny Kent diligently compiled her 'budget', Miss Clayton wrote to our mother, whom she called Mrs Cary, while she and our father were away. This letter survives, revealing the eternal struggle between siblings. This time it was over the sweet box.

My dear Mrs Cary,
…Bobby is trying very hard to live up to your last injunctions. There were great heart-burnings over the last candy-kiss in their sweet box and I wrote their names on scraps of paper and Bobby picked and got his own name so he had the sweet. Afterwards going to his rest, he said, "I was awfully frightened it was going to be Jean at first and then Pat. But I'm so glad they didn't get it. At least, I aren't, because Mummy said we were to be kind to each other."
Yours lovingly,
Enid Clayton.

It seems that my little brother had as much trouble being good to his siblings as I did.

Miss Clayton's methods were more modern than Miss Harrison's, but even so she could only take our education so far. After a while, it was decided that I would share a governess with a small number of girls of my age who lived nearby. My classmates were Dorothy Robinson, Anne Freeman, Rosemary Daniel and Anne White, whose father was commander of the Lancaster barracks. We met at Dorothy Robinson's house at Salt Oke, to take lessons with Miss Bayliss. Townson would drop me off on his way back from dropping off our father at the train station for his morning commute into Preston.

Jean sometimes came along for the ride and while we older girls had lessons, she would be taken for walks and help Dorothy Robinson's grandmothers Mim and Blousie in the garden. She remembers being allowed to pull up the weeds, which fitted perfectly with Jean's helpful nature and love of the outdoors. She was a Brownie Guide by then and I remember her singing a little ditty as she went about her day, 'Here we are the sprightly sprites, as brave and helpful as the knights'. The sprites was the name of her brownie guide 'six'.

Later Jean had lessons with our friend Joy Welch. The Welches were our nearest neighbours and we often spent time with them. Whenever the weather permitted, we would play tennis on their court, under the watchful eye of the Welches' grandmother, who had asked that the fences around the tennis court be taken down so that she could see the children play. We didn't miss the fences until a ball went out and bounced far out of sight. That didn't happen too often. The Welches' tennis court was notoriously boggy and our Uncle Bill complained that if he served too hard, the ball would just get stuck in the ground when it hit the other side of the court.

It was at the Welches' house that Jean and I got to hear all the latest music. At Newland, Grandboffin had sole control of the radio dial and there was no question of his wanting to listen to Children's Hour. Neither were we able to listen to dance music shows such as that presented by Henry Hall, which we loved.

Jean and I both enjoyed dancing and took ballroom lessons at a dance school in Preston. The teacher had her favourites, and we often spent half the lesson watching 'Lorna and Anne alone' (with the emphasis on 'alone') spinning around the floor while the rest of us seethed with resentment on the side-lines. I think we were supposed to be looking on in awe!

We didn't have a television in those days but we often went to the cinema with the Welch children. Jean and I were mad about the movies. In 1936, a lovely new cinema – the Odeon – opened in Lancaster, in a beautiful art deco building. It was a great treat to see a film there. The opening programme at the new cinema featured 'Mr Deeds Goes To Town' starring Gary Cooper and Jean Arthur, but our first trip to the Odeon was in the company of Joy Welch to see the children's classic 'Little Lord Fauntleroy', adapted from the novel by Frances Hodgson Burnett, with Freddie Bartholomew in the title role. Jean and I both loved the story of the young American boy who discovers he is heir to a British fortune. The idea of inheriting a fortune rather appealed.

I continued my education under Miss Bayliss until I was 14 years old. My parents had decided to delay my being sent to boarding school until my brother Bob was also ready to go away. When I turned 14, Bob was still only seven, but in those days, that was considered the perfect age for a young boy to be sent away from home. Our parents chose Packwood Hall for Bob (the headmaster had been at Shrewsbury School with our father). Looking for a girls school nearby, my parents settled on The Laurels, in the grounds of Wroxall Abbey. At long last I was off.

CHAPTER SEVENTEEN

Jean

The year of the coronation was a particularly important one for Lancaster. In 1937, the town was finally awarded the status of a city.

The award was not expected. Though Lancaster had always felt like quite the metropolis compared to sleepy Dolphinholme, it did not by any means reach the criteria for city status set by the Home Office in the early 1900s. It did not, for a start, have a big enough population – the baseline being 250,000, while Lancaster at that time had fewer than 52,000 residents. However the town did have one reason to be hopeful that its petition might be granted. Our new King George VI also carried the title 'Duke of Lancaster'.

That royal connection proved key and on May 5th, 1937 the King gave his assent to Lancaster becoming a city, prior to a grant being made on Coronation Day. The King's private secretary wrote that George VI 'feels that the long association of Lancaster with the crown would justify a departure from the rule'.

The local paper reported on the joyful news, which was made public at a ceremony on Giant Axe, Lancaster's football ground. The report said:

'Though the weather on Coronation-day in Lancaster

was not as genial as had been hoped, it in no way damped the ardour or enthusiasm of its citizens, who, one and all, rejoiced in the fact that from that day forward, their town had become a city.

'The official announcement that His Majesty the King had been pleased to honour the capital of the County Palatine in this signal fashion on his coronation day gave unbounded satisfaction to all ranks of the people and gave an impetus, if such were needed, to the display of loyalty and enthusiasm which marked the day's programme.

'In the morning, thousands of people assembled on Giant Axe to witness the breaking of the Royal Standard, and the loyal tribute of the troops from the Depot Kings' Own Regiment, the 350th Battery Royal Artillery, and the 5th Battalion of the King's Own Regiment. Subsequently, in various parts of the town, bands played and in the afternoon, field displays were held on Giant Axe and other enclosures for the entertainment of the schoolchildren, who afterwards partook of tea at their respective schools, where they received their Coronation souvenirs. In the evening, the Giant Axe was the scene of another giant display in which old and young participated, concluding with a display of fireworks. At the churches, in the morning, there were appropriate services, and at the Cathedral, High Mass was celebrated by the Bishop of Lancaster, the Right Rev T W Pearson.'

The letters patent making Lancaster's new city status official were read aloud on May 26th and plans were put in motion for a week of celebration in September.

On the first day of that September week thousands of commemorative silver spoons were distributed to Lancaster's children, with two further identical spoons being sent to the Princesses Elizabeth and Margaret at Buckingham Palace. On the second day, Lancaster's secondary school pupils lined the route of a civic procession led by the band of the 5th Battalion of the King's Own royal regiment to the priory and parish church, where a service was held ahead of the unveiling of a plaque by the Chancellor of the Duchy of Lancaster. That same day, a football team from Morecambe took on Lancaster in a commemorative football match and the Standfast works band led a concert.

There were similar festivities all week long but for us, the part we most looked forward to was the pageant, a grand outdoor historical procession, which took place on the Saturday afternoon. The 1937 pageant portrayed the history of the city from its earliest days as a settlement of Ancient Britons. There were episodes on the Roman occupation, on John of Gaunt, on George Fox (founder of the Quakers, who spent time in Lancaster prison) and on Queen Victoria's visit to the city in 1851. The pageant followed Lancaster's story right up to the moment when the new city was given its charter.

We were terribly proud when our father was chosen to play Bonnie Prince Charlie, son of the exiled Stuart King James VII and II, who catalysed the Jacobite Uprising when he returned from France to Scotland to reclaim the crown for his father. As children, Pat and I were very keen on the legend of the Bonnie Prince and often played at being

Jacobites in our 'pretends'. This was possibly inspired by our father's first outing as the Young Pretender, which took place at the Lancaster pageant of 1930.

It was a great thrill to us to think of our father as the prince again, though in all likelihood he was cast in the part because he was the only local man willing to ride a horse in a kilt. Sandy, our father's horse, was pressed into service too.

Bob and I took part in a different episode of the pageant. Together with our friend Joy Welch, we played three of Queen Victoria's many children. We were very pleased to be driven around Lancaster in an open carriage, waving at the crowds in imitation of Queen Mary, who had once waved to us as the Royal Car sped by.

There were 21 episodes to the pageant in all, with a script written by the Rev Harold Hastings, who acted as pageant master. More than 1,200 local people took part, along with a large number of horses (the Lancashire Mounted Constabulary played the Romans), oxen and even a pack of wolfhounds. The Band of the King's Own Royal Regiment provided musical accompaniment.

At the end of the pageant, the participants and the crowd gathered to sing 'O God Our Help in Ages Past' and the national anthem, led by one Miss Dorothy Seward on her new-fangled microphone.

Pat did not attend the celebrations that day, having already left for school. Our mother was also away at the time, staying in Bath with our grandfather, Pops, so the day after all the excitement, I wrote her a letter, signing off with my nickname, Jinks.

Darling Mummy,

Thank you awfully for the post-card. The pageant went off very well, it rained a bit in the morning but cleared up in time. Robert looked sweet in his kilt and Daddy was very posh too, and tremendously admired. I had a lovely green silk dress with pink frills and a bonnet to match. Joy had a mauve dress with pink frills too. We both had dark green coats with a fringe and sleeves (sewn on inside) to match our frocks. It was awful fun. We went round the town in Morecambe coaches with very posh coachmen and two guards and some very old-fashioned policemen. Daddy was two episodes in front of us and his Pipers kept on all the time. Miss Clayton photo-ed us lots of times and a man from the Yorkshire Post took Daddy and Bobby and me so I want to get it.

It is lovely and sunny today and Miss Clayton and me biked to church. I'm longing to see you again. I better stop now so thank you again for your postcard, with heaps of love from Jinks.

Thus, Lancaster celebrated becoming a city in the most perfect way.

CHAPTER EIGHTEEN

Pat

Since the days when Jean and I played 'pretends' in the nursery at Newland Hall, I'd been very interested in acting and the theatre. I was terribly envious of my sister and Bob, playing Queen Victoria's children in that 1937 pageant, but I had my own opportunities to take to the stage. At a previous local pageant, themed around Alice In Wonderland, I'd played Alice herself, decked out in a dress sewn by our mother to match the illustrations in the book. In that same entertainment, Jean and Bob had played two of the playing card soldiers who accompanied the Queen of Hearts. They certainly looked the part in their costumes but unfortunately Bob was struck with stage-fright and refused to go on unless he was accompanied by his nanny, Nana Mackenzie, who was rather incongruous among the brightly-dressed children in her long black coat and matching hat.

As a teenager, I was a girl guide and enjoyed taking part in all their activities, from camping to church parade. I was very pleased to be made a sixer. My pack took part in a pageant, bringing together all the local guide troops, to celebrate the coronation year. It took place at the Ripley Hospital in Morecambe, in the June of 1937, and I played the 'Spirit of Youth Down the Ages'. My costume, made by our mother again, was a vaguely 'Ancient Greek' affair, with a white cloak and draped white skirt. In my hand, I carried a wand.

'The Spirit of Youth' was an important part with several lines in a number of scenes. Unfortunately – possibly because I was simultaneously rehearsing for a part in another play, of which more later – I found it strangely difficult to commit those lines to memory.

I would stride out onto the stage, raise my wand and intone, 'I am the spirit of youth down the ages and I stand here…' Suffering a mental blank. That was what I was standing there doing.

I was very worried that I would forget my lines on the day of the actual performance, but I rose to the occasion and scribbled on my copy of the script, 'I remembered my part on the day. It went off as well as possible, seeing as it poured pretty steadily throughout. We nearly had to abandon it!'

The other play, which was obviously taking up more of my memory at the time, saw me in a very different role.

Our father was a lynchpin of the local amateur dramatic scene and I had been invited to take part in his company's production of 'The Bathroom Boys', a one-act play in which several gentlemen share comic banter as they wait in line to use a bathroom, thinking that it's occupied by a particularly selfish chap, only to discover they have been waiting for a woman to finish her luxurious bath. I played the woman.

I wrote about the rehearsals and the performance in the Ashton Hall of Lancaster's Town Hall in my diary.

April 18th. Sunday.

I have been having awful fun this week. On Friday I went (with Daddy and Mummy and Jean and Jill) to the Ashton Hall, at about 6.30pm. Parked our coats downstairs and went to the main hall, where the British Industries Touring Bazaar was going on.

We went to the Committee Room where they do plays, and Mummy went off with Jean and Jill and I watched The Bathroom Boys rehearse. There was Daddy, Mr Adams, who goes about in a special railway coach seeing lines, Mr Drummond, who is a school-master and plays the piano and is going to be married in the summer, Mr Edwards, who was Mr Barrett in the 'Barretts of Wimpole Street' and Mr Stansby, who is very nice and I once did polka with him at a dance. They did the end bit, where I come in smoking a cigarette through a long holder, for my benefit, and then we went and dressed. I had the Mayor's robing room all to myself, and they had the council chamber.

When the house was full we all went across to the back of the stage (which is extremely small but has very bright footlights and headlights) and Mr Adams gave me a box of chocolates and two film magazines and I sat on the only chair behind and the concert began and they went on. I saw a lot of it through a hole in the scenery. It was all about five people waiting outside the bathroom for a very tiresome young man who had been in for hours to come out. They sang songs and Mr Edwards did a lovely imitation of Mrs Hoyle and Daddy came and lighted my cigarette and when they said '…locked the door', I came out, all dressed up in chiffon pyjamas and silk dressing-gown and high-heeled shoes and lipstick and nail polish and carrying a towel and chocolates and magazines and Grandboffin's sponge and smoking the cigarette through the long holder and said, very haughty, 'I've finished my bath now. Do any of you want a bath?' Then I nearly giggled… and they switched off the lights and pulled down the curtain. We went back and changed, and had a lovely supper in the banqueting hall and Mr Welch bought me a lovely bouquet and we went home and got into bed at about 10.15.

Yesterday we went to the town hall at about 5.30pm and our first performance was at 6.30. As it takes about 45 minutes, there was very little time between that and the next, which was at 7.30. At the end of the 7.30 one Mr Adams presented me with the box of chocolates on the stage, and then we changed and all the cast with their wives and the Welches and Mrs Oglethorpe whose loathsome children were romping round with the little Stansbys, had supper together, and then we went home and got into bed about 11pm. I am rather sleepy this morning, as the time has gone on an hour, and I have a sore throat. The others are at church. I wish I didn't have that dreamy feeling nearly every time anything nice happens, and I am at all excited. Last night everything was very unreal.

Our father Cary was much in demand for the local entertainments. He once sang with Thora Hird, the famous Lancashire comedienne.

He appeared in amateur performances of 'Rose-Marie' and 'The Desert Song', in which he played the enigmatic hero the Red Shadow. During our childhood, he often sang for us at home, accompanied by our mother or Jean on the piano. On those happy family occasions, none of us could have begun to imagine how important our father's talent for entertaining would be during his time as a prisoner of war.

After serving with the Royal Marines in the Great War, our father remained in the Territorials. When war was declared in September 1939, his regiment – the 137th Field Regiment – immediately began training to be sent to the front line. In 1941, they sailed from Liverpool to the Far East to defend Singapore. When Singapore fell to the Japanese in February 1942, the men of our father's regiment were interned along with thousands of others in the Chungkai prisoner of war camp in Thailand. As he was one the more senior-ranking officers taken captive, the Japanese entrusted our father with the role of the camp's British commandant.

The men of the 137th spent three long years in Chungkai, during which time they were set to work on the 260-mile-long Siam-Burma (Thailand-Myanmar) railway, which included the notorious 'Bridge Over The River Kwai' (which our father thought was a very good film if entirely inaccurate). Conditions were harsh and many thousands of Allied prisoners died of illness and malnutrition. Many more died at the hands of the Japanese guards, who were brutal in administering punishment for the slightest infraction.

There wasn't a great deal our father could do to improve

the material situation for his fellow prisoners but he understood the importance of keeping morale high and thus he turned to his love of singing and drama. He discovered among his men a good number of amateur actors and musicians – and some professional artists too. Together they built a makeshift stage on which they put on shows for their fellow prisoners. The entertainments were equally popular with the Japanese guards, who would sometimes join the prisoners in the audience.

Years later, when preparing our father's memoir, '1,000 Days on the River Kwai', for publication, Jean and I found letters from some of his campmates, including A.B. Miller, who wrote, 'One of my own vivid personal memories was of one evening returning to Chungkai after an exhausting day on the railway, and joining hundreds of others enjoying an 'impromptu' concert, the 'star item' being Cary Owtram, with his beautiful tenor voice, dressed as the Red Shadow singing excerpts from 'The Desert Song'.

CHAPTER NINETEEN

Pat

In September 1937, I headed off to The Laurels, a girls' boarding school housed in a large Victorian house built in the ruins of Wroxall Abbey near Warwick.

Wroxall Abbey was once the country estate of Sir Christopher Wren, architect of St Paul's Cathedral. The main house is now a hotel but in the grounds still stands the Lady Chapel, the Church of St Leonard, commonly known as 'Wren's Cathedral'. While Wren didn't build the chapel, he did redesign its interior and his wife and other family members are buried there. The chapel is now a cathedral of the Communion of Evangelical Episcopal Churches. In 1937, it was where we had school prayers.

Arriving at the imposing Gothic building that housed my new school all those years ago, I couldn't help but be a little nervous. My nervousness only increased as I waited to meet my new classmates and find out where I would be sleeping. Dormitories had been carved out of the bedrooms of the main house and they were all different sizes. To begin with, I was given a bed in a room shared with seven other girls. One of them was very lively and after lights out on my first night, she proposed loudly, 'Let's smash up all the old school furniture!' I was terrified by the prospect but thankfully, the other girls in the dorm were equally appalled at the idea and the smashing of furniture did not go ahead.

Though I did my best to settle in, I quickly felt quite homesick. I tried hard to combat the feelings, writing in my diary, 'When I am feeling my most homesick and mis I either think of the lime trees by the gate in Blair Atholl, which I can smell if I shut my eyes, or that glimpse of hills one can get from my bedroom window.'

I felt lonely. I was also very frustrated. School was not at all how I had expected it to be. At home, I had reached an age where, if my mother was otherwise engaged, I was trusted to receive visitors and preside at tea parties. Now here I was being treated like a child again. It didn't help that my governess-led education had left me ahead in some subjects but quite behind in others. I enjoyed English, which was taught by Miss Gray, but I found it difficult to catch up with my classmates in maths and had to have extra lessons with one or two other girls. Likewise, to begin with I was behind the rest of the class in Latin.

I also found it harder than I had expected to make friends in those early weeks. Most of the girls in my class had already been at the school for a couple of years before I arrived and they had formed tight little friendship groups that were difficult to break into. I remember feeling slightly awed by Joan Parker, the head girl, who seemed to be good at everything. I was very glad when later in my first term another new girl – Mary Shaw – arrived and she and I were able to pair up together. We got along very well and I stayed with her in North Wales during the holidays.

We were well taken care of at The Laurels. The school was overseen by two headmistresses, Miss Rutter and Miss Jolly, whom we called 'the Nut' and 'the Bird'. Miss Rutter (the Nut) was stern and solemn, but Miss Jolly (the Bird) was softer and kinder.

All our meals were prepared for us and we didn't have to bother ourselves with laundry either. But we wanted to know how to look after ourselves. A number of us asked for cookery lessons but were told that wasn't part of the curriculum. I suppose that reflected the roles we were expected to play post-education: roles similar to those our mothers and grandmothers inhabited. Wives, mothers and hostesses. I did have a sense that we were missing out on some things that would be useful in adult life. Looking back, I can see that the curriculum was fairly narrow on all fronts. As Jean later put it, 'We were only taught the "best bits" of history. The bits where we were winning.'

One thing about being at The Laurels that pleased me very much was that it was so near to Stratford-upon-Avon, which meant we were regular visitors to the theatre there.

During my first year, we were taken to see 'The Tales of Hoffman' and 'The Mikado', which I enjoyed. We also saw 'The Tempest', though I wrote in my diary that the performance seemed unremarkable since I had been lucky enough to see John Gielgud play Shylock in 'The Merchant of Venice' while visiting Uncle Tom and Aunt Gioia in London. I was becoming a tough critic.

In July, I joined a school group on a trip to see a pageant

at nearby Kenilworth. It turned out to be unintentionally hilarious in parts. The pageant was performed in the ruins of Kenilworth Castle, which had been brilliantly lit for the purpose with big arc lights.

As one might expect in England in high summer, the weather threatened to cancel the outdoor show, but though we arrived in a shower, the rain cleared and the pageant began with a loud fanfare of trumpets. The first episode was a bucolic scene, incorporating a real flock of sheep. Then came a wedding procession, all on horseback, which is where the trouble began. While the cast of the pageant might have been excellent actors, competent riders they were not, and they could not keep the horses from prancing away from the microphones while they tried to deliver their lines.

It got worse. There was one horse in particular that seemed determined to steal the show. First it dragged the poor chap playing Simon De Montfort, 6th Earl of Leicester, off through the bushes, while he clung miserably to its mane, then, repurposed as Young Prince Edward's trusty steed, it cantered back on stage with a wicked glint in its eye. I described the ensuing chaos in a letter to my parents.

… Young Prince Edward appeared round the corner which Simon had just departed by, with his army. Well if that was all he could raise he must have been nearly as witless as the clan Montfort. However, he talked pretty into a microphone and seemingly didn't notice that the castle gates were open and quite undefended till a female called Maggot, who said she was in Lurve with Young Prince Edward (who replied

with gratified surprise, "Ooh, are you?") pointed this out to him. YPE then said that they must go into ambush, and proceeded to mount his horse. However, it was rather fresh (which was surprising seeing it had already been ridden by Simon and one of the wedding and would appear in almost every ensuing episode) and sidled round and round with the miserable YPE hopping after it with one foot in the stirrup.

Meanwhile the de Montfort contingent, carefully timed, appeared round the other side of the castle and were not unnaturally somewhat surprised to find Edward and friends still in possession of the stage. However, with some presence of mind, they fled to the castle and poured in through the gates, and slammed same. One of them was left outside, having arrived late, however he gave the gates a gentle push and they promptly swung open and engulfed him, and Edward's complete army managed to collectively hold his charger long enough for him to mount, and exeunt omnes gallopentes.

I recounted the rest of the pageant in some detail – several pages in fact – before interrupting the comedy with an observation that seems like an omen now.

It is very thundery here with constant cloud-bursts. The Territorials or something are doing military manoeuvres round and about. There were absolute volleys of machine-gun fire all this morning.

I didn't dwell on it, moving on to more school news:

We had a bottle of cider left over after the staff party, which, with large quantities of food also left over, we stored in our form room cupboard. So last night we brought out the intoxicating liqueur and were jubilantly swilling it out of tooth-glasses, when we heard The Nut escorting some visitors round. So we hastily stowed it away but there was a terrific reek of cider when they came in, I hope they didn't suspect anything.

Tons and tons of love, Patricia Owtram.
(PS. You can still call me Pat – this is me practising my flourishing signature)

Keen to make my mark as a writer, I became editor of the school magazine, which was called 'The Laurel Leaf'. The magazine had been in existence for a while but mostly concerned itself with sporting results. I tried to change its remit somewhat, asking my fellow pupils to submit poems (I was still writing my own), stories and articles, to supplement the usual hockey reports.

Though I did enjoy hockey and often played for the school, I much preferred tennis. The games mistress put me in a foursome with a French girl, a Danish girl and another girl, an Austrian refugee. The atmosphere on the court was very tense as the Danish girl came from a fascist family and made no secret of her disdain for our Jewish teammate. I found the Danish girl's position incomprehensible, knowing what I did by then of the plight of the Jewish community in Germany and Austria.

CHAPTER TWENTY

Pat

At the weekends, we Laurels girls were allowed to have visitors, who could take us out of school for the day. I looked forward to these visits very much indeed. One glorious February weekend, my parents picked me up on Saturday morning and took me to Birmingham, where we went to the British Industries Fair, an exhibition centre showcasing British industry, craftsmanship and design. Built in the 1920s, it had quickly become the most visited attraction in Britain. I described it as 'very interesting but tiring'. The highlight for me was getting into the exhibitors' dining room after my father borrowed an exhibitor's badge from a friend.

I had to return to school for the night, but on Sunday morning, my parents came to fetch me again for a day trip to Bath, where we had lunch with Pops at the hotel where he was living at the time. On the way back, we had tea at Stratford, which left us running a little late for my return to school and I wrote in my diary that we were 'gonged' by a police-car for exceeding the 30 mile an hour limit on the return drive.

Running perilously late would become a theme of my years at The Laurels. Apart from family members, I often received visits from Gwen Webb-Peploe. Gwen was a great friend of our mother's. They'd known each other since they were young girls in Preston. During the First World War, Gwen had worked in Manchester Hospital, where she became a very well-respected member of the nursing staff.

I remember Gwen as a rather forceful sort of person, quite tweedy and bossy but always well-meaning. The daughter of Canon Frances Hanmer Webb-Peploe, she had a traditional ecclesiastical upbringing, but she also had something of a rebellious streak about her that set her apart from most women of her social standing.

Gwen was an accomplished horsewoman, who kept shire horses. She was very involved in their upkeep and breeding and caused a small scandal when she took one of her horses – a mare called Bonny – to stud. Never in the history of the stud farm had a mare been brought by a woman. It was considered most unseemly for a woman to be involved in the business of animal husbandry. To make matters worse, Gwen insisted on staying to watch while Bonny was served by an enormous Wyresdale.

Gwen raised eyebrows once more when she took the resultant filly to a horse show in London. Showing shire horses was very much a masculine pursuit and no lady had ever taken a horse into the Agricultural Hall. As a result, the stewards didn't quite know what to do with Gwen. There was a well-established dress code for such events but it had not been written to accommodate female owners. In the end, Gwen wore a skirt over her jodhpurs and her foal won ninth prize.

Gwen's maverick ways were still very much in evidence when I started boarding school. Coming to take me out on a Sunday afternoon, she would turn up in her little car and whisk me away to a tea house in Warwick or to her nearby mediaeval cottage, which was called Att-ye-Crosse.

It was wonderful to spend time with Gwen – she even let me smoke some of her Balsam Sobranies – but as the afternoon went on, I would begin to get anxious. We boarding pupils had a very strict curfew – especially on Sundays – but Gwen took the time at which I had to be back at school as a suggestion rather than a diktat I knew it to be. She was excruciatingly casual about it, taking her time over tea, while I was hopping up and down with anxiety. I would get terribly worried as the minutes ticked by and Gwen showed no sign of intending to get me back to The Laurels. We would inevitably screech into the drive, 15 minutes late, to find the Bird waiting on the school steps, ready to give me a ticking off. When Jean arrived at the Laurels two years later, Gwen would get her into trouble too.

After I left school, Gwen continued to keep an eye on me. During the Second World War, she was often in London, acting as companion and social secretary to Lady Cynthia Elwes. I was always glad to get an invitation to Lady Cynthia's house for tea. Not least because the comings and goings of the staff there provided much entertainment.

I was enormously fond of Gwen. She took great interest in me and my siblings and we were always glad to see her. She was always kind and generous. I am sure, however, that there were people who saw her – a spinster of a certain age – as a figure deserving of pity.

The Great War, which had claimed the lives of so many young men, had put paid to the marital prospects of many women of Gwen's generation. They were known unkindly as 'surplus women' or 'excess girls'. It was estimated that there were some 250,000 more single women than men and their fate was agonised over by the newspapers of the time.

I like to think that most of those surplus women were happy pursuing their passions in the wider world without having to worry about hurrying home to attend to a hungry husband and children, but perhaps even Gwen – despite her horses – felt lonelier than I imagined. While I was still at school, she confided in me that she was thinking of becoming a nun, something which made me very sad at the time. I didn't want to lose my friend. She did attend Stanbrook Abbey in Worcestershire, in the hope of taking her vocation there. It wasn't to be.

Gwen came to stay at Newland Hall in 1959, which was unfortunately to be the last year of her life. Over the years she had sustained a number of injuries which might have contributed to her early death. She had been trampled by a horse and also got glass in her eye during the Blitz, an injury from which she never fully recovered. In the end, she had a form of stroke while staying at Green Leaves, a hotel near Steyning in Sussex. She was found unconscious in the morning and taken to hospital. She did not regain consciousness, but she was given the last rites. Our mother kept Gwen's last letter to her along with a series of letters of condolence written by Gwen's friends from all over the world, that are testament to how well-loved she had been. Jean and I still talk about her often, and remember with fondness those nerve-wracking moments when she made us late for school.

CHAPTER TWENTY-ONE

Jean

As the public agonising over the lives of the 'surplus women' showed, the social structures of the '20s and '30s were very rigid and there was little room for eccentricity.

One of the most well-known characters to be seen about Lancaster during our childhood was a man named Edgar Potts. Whenever we were in town with our mother, Edgar would be sure to pop up at some point, waving enthusiastically to attract our mother's attention.

As children we giggled discreetly with each other whenever Edgar appeared but despite his effusive manner his story, when we came to know it, was terribly sad. Edgar was born in the summer of 1899, at Hale in Cheshire, to a family he described in an account of his life which he wrote for me in later years, as 'ordinary middle-class people'. His mother's side were in business. His father's side were architects. Edgar's account recalls an early childhood full of visits to see chamber concerts and pantomimes. He had a love of music and also developed a great interest in the fashions of the day, observing 'clothes and appearances count'. However young Edgar's life changed forever when he was sent away to boarding school. He skips over those years, saying only, 'My school days were not happy, through running up a few bills it was eventually decided to put me away and the next 36 years were spent as a private patient at the Royal Albert Institution, Lancaster, for the feeble-minded of the Northern Counties. In those days it was much easier to be certified than now.'

Edgar was just 16 years old when he was admitted to the Royal Albert Institution for reasons we can still only guess at. It seems preposterous today that 'running up a few bills' would be enough to land a teenager in an institution for most of his adult life. Yet apparently that is what happened.

Edgar's fate was not entirely unusual for the early 20th century. Young people – women in particular – were often 'put away' for spurious reasons. For the most part, the being sent away was not for the benefit of the patient but to spare their middle and upper-class families the embarrassment of being associated with a family member who didn't conform to strict social mores. In his account, Edgar refers to 'an Eton boy who robbed the tuck shop' as having been institution-alised at around the same time.

Edgar did not have a happy time at the Royal Albert Institution, which was run by a medical superintendent who seemed especially unkind. Edgar wrote, 'On one occasion I wished him a Merry Christmas; he told me to go away, he did not want my good wishes! He always addressed me as Potts, I hated my own name.'

Fortunately, other members of the staff were kinder. Edgar was set to work in the Institution's printing shop and liked his boss there – 'A fine character with a keen sense of humour.' The matron too was a kind woman, who took Edgar out on many trips and visits. It must have been on one of these trips that Edgar first met our mother.

Edgar wrote in the account he gave me, 'The local gentry gradually heard of me. Miss Alice Haines, a friend of our matron, introduced me to Mrs Cary Owtram, a real saint. The sound of her voice always thrills me, she was the first to get permission to take me out. We have spent many happy times together. When her father – Colonel Charles Daniel – died they allowed me to attend his funeral. She was dressed entirely in white.'

It is typical of our mother that even at a time of great personal sadness, she thought to include Edgar, knowing how much it would mean to him to be among the 'gentry' of which he was so keen to be a part.

Through our mother, Edgar met a great many interesting people. Our Aunt Ellie wrote, after meeting him, that she was certain he was much nicer and more capable than many people outside the gates of the institution. He was invited to stay with our mother's friend Mrs Elletson at Parrox Hall, one of the oldest family houses in Lancashire. 'A delightful house,' Edgar called it. 'One sleeps in a four-poster bed and the whole atmosphere permeates elegance.' He also became friends with Brigadier and Mrs Fitzroy Maclean.

Major-General Sir Fitzroy Maclean, as he became, was another local celebrity. In the 1940s and '50s, he was MP for Lancaster, but prior to that, he'd had a very interesting and adventurous life. In the late 1930s, he'd been a diplomat in the Soviet Union, but left the diplomatic service at the outbreak of the Second World War so that he might join the army. During the war he headed up the British military mission to Yugoslavia, serving as Winston Churchill's personal representative to Tito, leader of the Communist Partisans, with whom he had a particular rapport. Maclean's memoir, 'Eastern Approaches', documents those years. Suffice to say, Maclean's exploits were so heroic that he's rumoured to have been the model for Ian Fleming's infamous Agent 007, James Bond. I was lucky enough to be able to work with him, both during the war and afterwards, of which more anon.

Edgar wrote movingly of his battle to be allowed to leave The Royal Albert Institution, 'The Bishop of Lancaster... helped a lot, he and Fitzroy did so much to get my freedom.' Our mother also did what she could, signing up to be the person responsible for Edgar when he was allowed a holiday away from the RAI.

A change of Medical Superintendent at the institution and a Labour government, which brought in a bill providing assistance for the institutionalised to get away and lead a normal life also helped. Unfortunately, when Edgar Potts was finally discharged, his family were not keen to resume responsibility for him. He writes also of the unkindness of the chief attendant at the hospital who made him wheel his belongings – including Joey, his beloved budgerigar – through Lancaster on a hand cart to the station. Our mother stepped in to help and soon Edgar was found a place at the Friary of St Francis, near Cerne Abbas. There he found friendship with the brothers, while continuing to make connections with the great and the good. He picked primroses for Queen Mary, whose secretary wrote to say that the Queen had displayed them in her drawing room.

Throughout the years, Edgar continued to stay in touch with our mother, who invited him to stay at Newland Hall, where she threw him a party.

'Mrs Cary Owtram met me with the car... Jean and Bobbie both at home. The third day Mrs Cary motored me to Dolphinholme Church, where we saw her father's tombstone and oak chair and reading desk in the church, in memory of him and his brother, Harold Daniel. I cycled to Wyreside Franciscan Friary, ugly house and no atmosphere. Met many old friends in Lancaster. The dogs – Bunch, Rip and Joey are sweet. A fine day.

'The third day, took Joey for a walk round Dolphinholme Church, all the family picked masses of flowers for the party, in my honour, which were arranged in huge vases and bowls, all over the house. Mrs Cary made the scones herself; a perfect day with brilliant sunshine. Mrs W.M. Pye, Mrs Mount, Fitzroy and Mrs Maclean with Susan and Jeremy, Mrs Riddell, Mrs H. Elletson and Miss Dolly Philips, Peter Jackson and his wife, Grace Ellam, Miss Alice Haines, Miss Cook and Miss Buchan, Mrs Richmond, Pat, Jean and Bobbie all came.

'After dinner, Colonel and Mrs Owtram motored me to see the Morecambe illuminations, too wonderful for words. The first day, Mrs Cary, after breakfast, motored me to Garstang to catch the express bus to Poulton, a glorious day. Mrs Cary picked two lovely bunches of flowers to take for Aunts Emily and Gertrude.'

Eventually, one Dr Armstrong authorised Edgar's discharge from the Mental Deficiency Act, which gave him more freedom than ever. The day after his discharge, he spent with Miss Monica Fair, a cousin of our mother's, who had been one of her bridesmaids. Later, my mother threw another tea-party in his honour at Newland Hall.

Edgar remained a great friend of the family and our paths crossed on many occasions. The injustice of Edgar's being institutionalised so young was often on my mind during my career as a social worker. I often wondered what kind of life Edgar might have led had he been born a couple of decades later. Would he have been a fashion designer perhaps, gathering a glittering salon around him? Or the maitre d' of a wonderful restaurant or nightclub, knowing everything and everyone? All those years Edgar spent in an institution were a terrible waste. In my work I hope I honoured Edgar's memory in my determination to always respect the differences that make us human.

In 1964, Edgar invited me to his 65th birthday party – a very elegant affair, with a classical piano recital by his friend Alan Rowlands. Edgar being Edgar, had invited the great and the good, including a duchess. His friend Lady Cynthia had agreed to help him 'receive'. Unfortunately, Lady Cynthia was late. I wrote to my mother:

However, we all chattered like parakeets and ate buns and drank milky coffee, and Veronica arrived in a blue coat and skirt (but looking very nice), and Lady Evelyn Jones in trailing pink drapes, and then we had photographs, and finally settled down to a very nice relaxing, classical piano recital... In the very dramatic middle of which I suddenly saw, through the open door, Lady Cynthia tottering about absent-mindedly up the stairs.

You can imagine the susurrating – "she's come", "she's here", "Lady Cynthia's arrived" hissed all round the room, and Edgar advancing with his paw extended, beaming, and total reorganisation of chairs, and Margie beside me on the sofa saying "what a giggle-making situation" and beginning to shake and the Duchess preserving complete composure and concentration, and the unlucky pianist tinkly valiantly on.

Sandwiches and coffee were produced again, and Lady C carried on an audible flow of small talk with her neighbour, while beating time to the music with a bitten sandwich. It was all a little distracting but wholly in keeping... Edgar enjoyed it all enormously... A splendid Pottsian evening!

CHAPTER TWENTY-TWO

Pat

Through our early childhood, Anglo-German relations had been relatively calm, though of course the Great War was still fresh in the memories of the adults in our lives, especially Grandboffin's. He often led us children in a game we called 'Bombing the Germans' which involved throwing stones at the piles of junk that had been dumped in a nearby quarry. That game was *verboten* when cousin Jill came to stay with her German nanny.

Jean, Bob and I had grown up on the Great War stories of our elders and in our youthful naivety, we were rather envious of the adventures our parents and their friends seemed to have had. We couldn't imagine anything so exciting happening in our lives. Since Hitler had come to power however, international relations were suddenly much less relaxed. In 1937, our Uncle Godfrey returned from a skiing trip to Germany with unsettling news of having seen many 'semi-military' people in uniform around the resort. Later on the same trip, Godfrey asked for lobster in the hotel dining room, only to be told that all the lobster was already reserved for General Goering's party. Germany was repositioning herself as a major military power and didn't care who knew it.

Hitler's influence was making itself felt beyond Germany's borders too. His rhetoric was emboldening anti-Semites in Germany and her neighbour Austria and many Jewish families were reconsidering their future in both those countries and making plans to leave. Some of those families headed for Israel, others planned to join family members in the United States. Still others came to Britain. Meanwhile, German citizens living in Britain were heading in the opposite direction. In March 1937, I wrote in my diary:

There is a danger of war this spring, but a crisis is not expected till this autumn, Aunty Gioia says. Her German maid has suddenly been recalled, and this is the fourth one she knows who has had to go home suddenly. So she rang up a Cabinet person she knows, and told him, expecting he would laugh. He did not laugh.

A little later, I wrote:

I had such a funny dream, only the night before it was odder: Mussolini had come to lunch, and I was being very sweet to him. The night before that, I dreamt that war had been declared and was going on in Dolphinholme: and I was carrying dispatches in a very old Ford car (a pre-war model with no roof or brakes) from the school to Newlands over the Crag with Laurence Olivier and we could not stop the car.

Quietly, Britain prepared for war. Information shorts were

shown before films in the cinema. In April, we went to see 'Romeo and Juliet' with Leslie Howard and Norma Shearer at the Palladium in Lancaster. I wrote:

It was terribly, terribly good and terribly, terribly tragic. I loved the balcony scene and admire Leslie Howard almost as much as King Edward, but not quite. I also rather like Basil Rathbone, but that's apparently a very wrong sentiment... We saw a St John's Ambulance Air Raid Defence Film before, all about refuge-rooms and gas-masks. I had always regarded war as a distant though possible calamity, and not thought very much about it. That film gave me a bit of a shock – it somehow brought it nearer; supposing we did have to use those masks and the poison gas comes creeping down the stairs of Newlands. I had never thought of that before.

Neither Mussolini nor Laurence Olivier ever came to Dolphinholme but the war brought other new faces into our lives.

By the late 1930s, Grandboffin was finding it impossible to find local women who were willing to work as cook or housemaid at Newland Hall (under-parlourmaids and kitchen maids were long just a memory). Few young people were willing to live in a draughty old house in the middle of nowhere. If you wanted to go from Newland to Lancaster without a car, you had to walk a mile to the nearest bus stop. It was much too isolated for anyone who wanted to have a proper social life. After a disastrous experience with some Northumberland miners' daughters who were bored stiff and left immediately, Grandboffin discovered an agency in London which found jobs for Austrian Jewish people so desperate to escape the march of the Third Reich that they were willing to take domestic jobs deep in the English countryside. Grandboffin informed the agency of his requirements and we waited for a match.

'But these Austrian people,' said Grandboffin one day. 'Won't know which are the drinking-water taps.'

Two kinds of water came into our house in the North Lancashire countryside. The mains supply came from Thirlmere in the Lake District and was drunk, I am sure with perfect safety, by everyone else in the county; but because of something to do with the state of the pipes at Newland Hall, Grandboffin preferred the water from one of the springs on the hillside above the house, which he had piped to two of the tenant farms, a cottage, a cattle-trough and the home farm, finally to a tank in the attic and from there to taps in the upstairs and downstairs pantries and the scullery.

Many years later my brother-in-law had the courage to look into the tank and found green slime and a drowned mouse; and years later still, when my brother sold the house and the estate to new owners, an inspector reported that none of the water in the house was safe to drink. All the same, three generations of our family drank it and mostly lived to a good old age; perhaps we had the kind of immunity calves do to the infections on their home farms.

That day in 1937 Grandboffin produced some of the manila labels he used to tie to the pheasants he gave to people like the vicar at Christmas, and a German dictionary which must have belonged to one of my uncles, and I wrote on each label in carefully copied black letter the ungrammatical phrases, 'Wasser fur Trinken' and we tied them to the appropriate taps. Such a minor thing can alter the whole course of one's later life.

Shortly afterwards the first young Austrian women from the London agency arrived. As Grandboffin had predicted, the new arrivals did not speak English, and as I had discovered three words of German, I fell into a sort of role as interpreter, doing my best to help them settle in. First there was Sad Maria, who sighed so deeply when handing round vegetables we all felt miserable too, then flighty little Renata who soon left for the bright lights of London.

Then, in 1938, Edith 'Edie' Krochmalnik of Vienna, came to work as a housemaid, followed not long afterwards by her friend Cecelia 'Lilly' Getzl. Their arrival would change all our lives.

CHAPTER TWENTY-THREE

Jean

Edith Krochmalnik — our friend Edie — grew up in Vienna's Jewish quarter, where her family had an apartment in a large block built around a central square. Her aunts lived on a different floor in the same building and her best friend lived right opposite. They could wave to each other across the garden before meeting up to play.

As a young woman, Edie trained as a milliner and married Richard Krochmalnik. It wasn't a love match — Edie had previously fallen in love with an orthodox Jew but their marriage was forbidden by his mother. Though the marriage didn't last, Edie and Richard remained friends.

Edie might have stayed in Vienna forever, but by the late '30s the situation for Jewish Austrians had been deteriorating for some time. When she arrived at Newland, Edie told us about the Anschluss on the 13th March 1938, when the Federal State of Austria was annexed into the German Reich to form Hitler's 'Greater Germany'. She recalled how March 12th had been a perfectly normal day like any other but she woke on the morning of the 13th to see the red and white Nazi flag, with its ugly black swastika, flying from every building, while the streets were suddenly filled with men in quasi-military uniforms. When Edie and other members of her family were made to scrub the pavements by jack-booted goons, she knew that it was time to leave.

By then Edie's brother and father had already left Vienna. Her brother was a communist and before they came for the Jews, the Nazis had come for the communists. Edie's brother escaped capture only because their mother had a friend in the local chief of police, who warned her that a round-up was coming. That very same day, Edie's brother and father made their escape to Poland, where they joined members of their extended family in relative safety.

But of course, the Nazis would not stop at rounding up the communists and, with her brother and father safely out of the country, Edie began to make her own plans. She'd heard from several friends about an agency in London that was recruiting Austrian Jews for domestic work in the UK. In July 1938, she applied for work and her details were passed on to us. Our mother immediately wrote on Grandboffin's behalf with an offer of employment.

To Fraulein Edith Krockmalnik,

I have received your address through Miss Wroe. I understand you wish to obtain a position in England. We require a house-parlourmaid. We keep four servants: a cook, two house-parlourmaids, and a kitchen maid. Our family is as follows...

Having outlined the composition of the Owtram family, our mother finished with an apology that the nearest synagogue

Below: Ethel "Effie" Owtram paternal grandmother in Shepherdess costume

Above: Our parents Cary Owtram and Dorothy Daniel at their wedding in 1921, Uncle Bill front row, far right side

Below: "It might have been very much worse!" Dorothy, Patricia, and Bebe pushing Jean along at Scarborough c.1929

Above, left: Dorothy Owtram with Patricia and Jean c.1929

Left: Patricia, Jean and Bobby early 1930s

Above: Edith 'Edie' Krochmalnik

Above: Mother loved picnics at Wellington Wood, early 1950s

Above: Jean, S.O.E Italy 1944

Above: Patricia at SHAEF Autumn 1944

Right: Patricia with Aunt Gioia wearing the 'New Look' while attending a wedding in London, 1947

Below: Patricia's first car! "My mother helped me to buy it and it had a number plate of LFM 22, which she said stood for 'love from Mum'. It was the Morris Thousand that I tried to keep up with a sports car in!"

Left: Jean and her husband Mike Argles c.1960s

Below: Patricia with Ray Davies, her husband at a BBC Party 1960s

Below: Patricia at Mystic, Connecticut, October 1953

Above: Boonpong Sirivejjabhandu M.B.E who rsked his life in helping the prisoners of Chungkai, where my father was a POW Camp Commandant. He remained a lifelong friend of the Owtram family. Here visiting Newland in around the early 1960s

Above: Boonpong's obituary

Left: Patricia with Sir Patrick Moore celebrating the 200th episode of Sky At Night in the 1960s

Left: Producing University Challenge with Bamber Gascoigne at Granada television

Right: Patricia working as a BBC Television producer in the 1960s

Left: Patricia's BBC producer credit, 1973

Below: Patricia at work, 1970s

Top: Patricia and Jean at a podcast recording. *Photo: S.Rabas*

Above: Celebrating the publication of Codebreaking Sisters in London 2020

was some distance away. Neither could she promise that life at Newland Hall would be anywhere near as exciting as life in Vienna. Edie was undaunted. Our mother's letter enabled her to get a travel pass and with that in hand, she was on her way.

Edie did not like to talk about her escape from Austria. What we do know is that she travelled alone, having failed to persuade her mother and sister that they should come with her despite the growing danger at home. She knew that she absolutely did not want to travel through Germany, so she plotted a route that took her through Switzerland instead. She'd thought that she would encounter less trouble going that way, but found that anti-Jewish sentiment was just as strong among the Swiss border guards as the Austrians. They forced her to hand over most of the things she was carrying with her, leaving her with just a couple of family photographs that became her most treasured possessions.

After many days in transit, Edie arrived in London; tired and alone and not able to speak a word of English. While she didn't like to remember the journey as far as London, she often talked about the taxi driver who picked her up at the docks and took her to the Young Women's Christian Association hostel where she spent her very first night in England. Moved by Edie's plight, the taxi driver promised to return the following morning to take her to the station to catch a train onward to Lancaster. The kind man kept his word.

It must have been frightening for Edie to make that lonely journey all the way to Lancashire but to stay in Austria might have been tantamount to suicide. On November 9th 1938, the Jewish community was targeted again on Kristallnacht – the Night of the Broken Glass. During the hours of darkness between the 9th and 10th, 267 synagogues in Germany, Austria and the newly-annexed Sudetenland (formerly part of Czechoslovakia) were destroyed, 7,000 Jewish business-es were wrecked and more than 30,000 Jewish men were arrested and taken to concentration camps. For Edie, newly arrived in Britain, it was clear there was no going back.

Edie soon learned English and thankfully she liked living in the countryside, having always described herself as a 'Wald und Wiesen Madchen', a girl of the forest and meadows. There were hiccups however. One weekend early in Edie's time at Newland, our parents threw a fancy dress party. To their horror, one of the guests arrived dressed as Adolf Hitler – still a figure of fun to those Brits who didn't fully understand the chaos he was sowing. When she saw him, Edie straight away flew upstairs to her room and refused to come back down until the thoughtless guest apologised to her in person.

Edie considered our mother to be the perfect English lady, but was amused by the behaviour of some of the women she encountered in Lancaster. She often told the story of how, visiting Woolworths in the town centre, she was astonished to see a fight break out between two women in the middle of the store – one was having an affair with the other woman's husband – while all the while 'Little Sir Echo', an old chil-dren's song made famous by Elsie Carlisle, played on a dem-onstration record player in the background. Evidently, this was not the way women in Vienna behaved in public and it made a lasting impression. No brawling in the shops for the Viennese!

Edie settled into life at Newland Hall but the fate of the rest of her family was a constant worry. Her Viennese aunts all disappeared and what became of them was never known.

After fleeing to Poland, Edie's brother had travelled on to Sweden. Having arrived in Stockholm, he was arrested and sent back to Poland three times but was ultimately allowed to stay in Sweden after the local Jewish community guaranteed he would not be a burden on the state. He eventually married a Swedish woman and made his life there.

Edie's father was not so lucky. It was not until years after the war that she discovered what had happened to him. He had survived for most of the conflict, moving from Poland to Hungary, but as the end of the fighting drew near, he found himself caught in a round-up of Jews in Budapest. Tired by now of the endless petty humiliations heaped on him by the Nazi occupiers, he refused to get into a lorry, which would have taken him God only knew where. He was shot for making that stand.

News of Edie's father's death came from one of his friends, who had been caught up in the same round-up and taken to a concentration camp. The friend survived the camp and made a deposition to the Red Cross upon his liberation.

Thankfully, Edie's mother and sister did survive the war. They left Austria for Belgium but when war was declared and it looked certain that Belgium would soon be occupied, they finally joined Edie in England. The agency that had placed Edie at Newland Hall, found work for her mother and sister at the Duke of Devonshire's London house. Edie's sister married a local man but her mother never really enjoyed British life, forever missing the sophistication of Viennese café society. Britain just wasn't the same.

Eventually, Edie found she missed her family too much to stay in Lancashire and moved to London to be with them. She married and set up home in Wembley Park. She had a daughter called Jacqueline. Pat visited Edie in London and Edie often returned to Newland Hall, to see us, and to catch up with other old friends in Dolphinholme.

It was lovely, very many years later, to hear Edie's daughter Jacqueline say that Edie considered her time at Newland Hall to be very happy and that she'd enjoyed spending time with me and Pat and teaching us both to speak German. We certainly enjoyed spending time with her.

In the 1950s, Edie and her husband built themselves a house. They called their new home Newlands. And in 2022, the letter our mother sent offering Edie a job in the summer of 1938, which she once told her daughter was 'the difference between life and death', was put on display as part of an exhibition on the Second World War in the Lancaster City Museum. The exhibition was entitled 'Hinge Of Fate: Living with Uncertainty in 1942'. It seemed like fate indeed that Edie should have come into our lives.

CHAPTER TWENTY-FOUR

Pat

A short while after Edie arrived at Newland, she asked our mother if she might consider making a job offer to one of her friends, who had also decided it was time to leave Vienna. Her friend's name was Cecilie Getzl. Edie called her Lilly.

Persuaded that Lilly Getzl would be just the right person to complete the Newland Hall team, our mother wrote with an offer of employment. Lilly arrived in Lancashire on April 19th,1939. I was home from school for the Easter holidays at the time. I wrote in my diary, 'Lilly charming…'

We were very happy to have Edith and Lilly with us but the cook – 'mean, silly woman' – was not so welcoming, nailing a board across the fireplace in the servants' hall so that the Austrians could not have a fire, though she had one in her own bedroom. Fortunately, our mother was very good at brokering peace.

I got on very well with Lilly. Though she was almost 20 years older than I, we soon became friends. We spent many evenings together in the parlour off the kitchen when I was home from school. Lilly had brought with her from Austria a few German books and magazines and she let me read these and the closely written letters on thin paper from her relations in Europe to improve my vocabulary. But most of all we simply talked about her life in Vienna. I loved to hear about the concerts and parties there, which sounded so much more glamorous than anything that happened at Newland.

Lilly had a cousin who played violin for the Vienna State Opera. I was fascinated to hear that when musicians auditioned for the orchestra, they had to do so from behind a screen, so that the people judging their performance were not influenced by the way they looked. An eminently sensible way of doing things. It seemed to me that the Viennese went to the opera as often and easily as we went to the Odeon in Lancaster.

I was an impressionable teenager and our conversations opened up a romantic, sophisticated world a long way outside my experience. I wrote in my diary:

Have been talking to Lilly... Find German comes nearly as easy as English – easier, when talking to her. Shall miss her very much if only we ever get away from here. She is so sympathisch and intelligente...

...The Viennese have a wonderful gaiety, even in semi-darkness in a dreary attic, England on the brink of invasion and really no future for either.... Lilly and Edie are delightful to talk to – we talk utter nonsense mixed with very deep subjects, politics, philosophy, fairy-tales...

...I hope I won't forget all this. It is so easy, one forgets the understanding one had with old friends and the things

one shared with them. There is no time to look back, it should all be forward. Plans, not memories, Preparation, not reminiscence.

As I learned German, Lilly learned English. When I was at school and later, when I moved to London, Lilly and I would write to one another in German. She gave me a grounding in a colloquial form of the language that would prove very useful indeed when I joined the Wrens (Women's Royal Naval Service). But more than that, she was a great friend and mentor, someone to whom I could always turn when life seemed tough. I will never forget her kindness.

Lilly remained at Newland Hall for many years, before retiring to live in a cottage nearby. Over the years, she became one of our mother's most trusted and precious confidantes. Lilly passed away in October 1988. She has a memorial stone in the graveyard at St Mark's in Dolphinholme, with a view of the Lancashire fells that she came to love.

CHAPTER TWENTY-FIVE

Pat

Though there had been growing concern about Germany for some time, a pivot point came in 1938, when, having annexed Austria in the Anschluss, Hitler next set his sights on Sudetenland.

After the end of the Great War, the Allied Powers had negotiated a series of treaties designed to punish Germany for the conflict. The most famous of these treaties was the Treaty of Versailles, named for the former French royal palace in which it was signed.

The treaty demanded that Germany accept responsibility for the war and disarm to prevent further conflict. It laid out a schedule of punitive reparations, which would see Germany paying the Allied Powers 132 billion gold marks, which equates to more than £280 billion pounds in today's money. Despite that huge sum, certain Allied leaders, such as Marshal Ferdinand Foch of France, still thought the terms too lenient.

It is now widely believed that the terms of the treaty led to widespread resentment in Germany and enabled the rise of the Nazi party, by making it easier for Hitler to whip up support for his ideology.

The Great War treaties also saw Germany lose territory.

Sudetenland, which comprised those sections of northern Moravia and northern and west Bohemia in the shadow of the Sudeten mountain ranges, had a predominantly German population, but under the Treaty of St Germain, it became part of the newly formed Czechoslovakia. Thus more than 3,000,000 Germans found themselves under Czechoslovakian rule and they were not happy about it at all.

In the two decades that followed Sudetenland's absorption into Czechoslovakia, German nationalism gathered pace. In 1935, the Sudeten German Party, as the local Nazi party was called, won two-thirds of the Sudeten German vote, which made it the second largest party in the Czechoslovak parliament. Led by Konrad Henlein, the Sudeten Nazis began to agitate for Sudetenland to be reunited with Germany.

Though the Czechoslovak government allowed Sudetenland to become self-governing, this was not enough to satisfy the Third Reich. It wasn't long before many in France and Britain were convinced that the only way to avoid a second war was for Czechoslovakia to give up the disputed territory – to appease Hitler, as it were. At the Munich Conference, at the end of September 1938, France and Great Britain met with Italy and Germany to discuss the situation. The outcome was that Czechoslovakia was issued with an ultimatum on September 30th. It was to cede the Sudetenland to Germany by October 10th.

I was at school at the time – feeling homesick again – and was perhaps too distracted to understand the full import of the news. However, other members of our family had a much clearer understanding of why the annexation, which was part of a British government policy of appeasement with regard to Hitler, came to pass and why it seemed like the best course of action at the time.

Our mother's only sibling was Admiral Sir Charles Saumarez Daniel, our 'Uncle Tid'. He was married to Aunt Marjorie and they had one daughter, our cousin Valery – Val. Uncle Tid had served in the First World War, seeing action in the Battle Of Jutland. He was a career naval man. In 1938, he was the captain of HMS Faulknor, a Royal Navy Destroyer.

We saw Uncle Tid only rarely – he was often away at sea. Fortunately, like our mother, he was a great letter writer and so it's no surprise that when our mother asked for his thoughts on the likelihood of another war with Germany in 1938, Uncle Tid responded at length and with great consideration. Our mother kept this particular letter for the rest of her life. Uncle Tid wrote on paper with the HMS Faulknor crest, with the motto 'Ducit amor patriae', which means 'Led by love of my country'.

> *Rosyth c/o GPO London.*
> *8th October, 1938*

My Dearest Bunt,

Thank you so much for your letter, I was delighted to hear from you…

…Here are my views on the crisis, for what they're worth. In 1919 France wanted the Rhine as her frontier. We and America flatly refused, as it obviously conflicted

directly with the doctrine of self-determination. Instead, however, we agreed with America to guarantee France's new frontier. America then backed out of it, and we at once followed suit. France then had to look elsewhere for security and found it very conveniently in the new Czech State... Czechoslovakia was erected regardless of self-determination, but based on strategic frontiers, and France has consistently refused to press Prague to give the minorities a fair deal. France counted on Czechs holding up 30 divisions in the East if Germany was at war with her, and she concluded a definite treaty with Czecho. She also concluded the notorious France-Soviet pact.

In effect, French policy was to build up a faction against Germany in Eastern Europe; in other words, keep Germany down. While Germany was weak, no minorities in Czecho stood a chance; and Sudeten Germans, enlisted or conscripted in the Czech army, would be expected to fight other Germans just over the frontier. These Eastern pacts of France were full of danger to us, as they might well lead to war between France and Germany, we might be dragged in to save France, as we could never contemplate her defeat. Hence we might be involved in war over a question, where no single vital British interest was concerned, i.e. over a quarrel starting in Eastern Europe. We have consistently refused to guarantee Czecho... Our mistake has been in not pressing France in the past to make the Czechs settle their minority problem. Then Germany became powerful, and we got the crisis that everyone who'd studied the problem knew would arise.

To my mind Chamberlain handled it magnificently. It was obvious that the form in which "Versailles" had constructed Czecho was utterly untenable. German force was now demanding what should have been hers long ago given to justice. But this was the point where one had to consider whether Germany only wanted her minorities; or whether she was set on smashing Czecho completely, getting the whole of Eastern Europe into her power, ending up in the Ukraine, Turkey, Persia, India etc etc, the old "Drang Nach Osten" theory. If that was really her object (which I refuse to believe) we might conceivably have gone to war, not for "gallant little Czecho"... but to smash Germany, in effect, a preventive war.

Some statesmen... said that a preventive war is never justifiable; and to have embarked the British Empire on a preventive war with Germany now would have been criminal. Very well; no preventive war, therefore the Czechs must give up their minorities. So this they agreed, urged, quite rightly, by France and us. That settled the principle. Germany, of course, wanted quick results... hence the German ultimatum, and all the crises etc that ensued. But with the principle of partition settled, to have started a war over a question of time-table would have been incredible and Chamberlain was right over and over again to collect the four power conference at the last moment, and get an agreed time-table, hard as it was on the Czechs. But had he not done so there'd be no Czechs left at all! And even suppose we'd fought and beaten Germany (having involved all the world in the process) we were then bound to let Germany have such Sudetens as were left alive, as we'd already agreed to that in principle before the war started!

The thing's fantastic. I wonder how the British Fleet would have helped the Czechs. As Lord Chatfield said, we should have been like one watching a man (Czechs) in a lion's cage, and saying "never mind if he does eat you; I'm going to cut off his rations afterwards"!

I disliked the arrogance and blatancy of Hitler as much as anyone, but what were we like at Versailles 20 years ago? Anyhow, it was a triumph to get him to agree, and I firmly believe that we can at last start on appeasement in Europe. France and ourselves can look after ourselves in the West; we must be clear of all Eastern Entanglements. Russia, if she'll stop shooting her officers and put her defences in order, can look after herself alone. Anyhow, "it's a long long way" to Leningrad, as Napoleon found. The next thing is to get settled with Italy, with whom we ought never to have quarrelled. Musso is keen for it now, with reason.

With France and ourselves strongly armed, I believe we can really get an abiding settlement with Germany, and so (paradoxically enough) be able to start disarmament. But what our Foreign Office policy in the past has to answer for... The fact is we've rightly declined a preventive war with Germany, and must now try (admittedly because Germany has grown strong) to put right some of the injustices of the past. But our precious Foreign Office ... living in the 1900-1914 era, visualise a jolly good world war with Germany; just "to learn 'er"! Then presumably *a similar peace to the last, followed by another cracking good war in due course, & so on. They pass man's understanding.*

I have no feeling whatsoever that British honour has in any way whatever been sullied. We'd saved Czecho for the Czechs, and they must be content with that, & be thankful to be spared annihilation. Never, in any way, did we guarantee the Czech state as constructed at Versailles, for the simple reason that it was untenable. But, the danger of war over, our left-wingers, idealists, "Leaguists" and "what nots" start a clamour against Chamberlain, who is too big a man to go to the Country and knock out every opponent for the next five years. Thank goodness we're rid of Duff Cooper; a most ineffective 1st Lord. Let's hope we may now get a really useful politician.

Lack of Russian intervention amuses me. I firmly believe that nothing would have pleased Russia more than to have Britain, France, Germany, Italy, & anyone else who felt like it, involved in a war from which she herself would, in the event, have remained aloof: for the result might well have been the triumph of Bolshevism in Europe. Russia as our ally! What a thought! When everything for which Russia stands is, must be, inimical to the real interests of the British Empire. How short our memories are. And if she had come in on our side, I can imagine no war in which we would have had so much to lose from the victory of an ally

And as for the League?

In its present form dead beyond recall; for it never attempted its main task, which was to settle grievances.

Now we must endeavour to settle them outside the League. Unfortunately we all must be equally heavily armed in order to make our opinions carry equal might. But I think it can be done and I think Chamberlain can do it. Democracies have got to co-exist with totalitarian states; & to realise that one's own idea of government does not necessarily commend itself to the whole world. I believe a lasting peace can well be built up out of this circus, even though still more armaments are needed in the process; for no country really wants a war. But it will be a difficult process, & the least the opposition can do is not to make it more difficult. I remain convinced of one thing; there was no possible justification for involving the British Empire in war over the partition of Czechoslovakia; neither in our own interests, nor in our honour.

Two weeks ago today, I took my flotilla into Scapa Flow; and as I looked round that familiar waste of desolate land and water, I wondered what speech I could make to my men to fill them with enthusiasm for a war of whose origins they would know nothing, and the justice of which they might well doubt. We made all our preparations, and, in the end, no speech was necessary. As we left Scapa Flow on Thursday last, and the Pentland Firth was left behind, I felt that four years spent there, over 20 years ago, had not, perhaps, been wasted. I recalled to mind what Vernede, killed in 1917, wrote during the war: –

"Then to our children there shall be no handing of fates so vain – of passions so abhorr'd –

But Peace... the Peace which passeth understanding...
Not in our time, but in their time, O Lord."

So, perhaps, our Bobbies, Vals, Pats, Jeans etc may still
have a chance of a saner and more wholesome world; not
at the expense of Czecho, but by a redress of some of the
wrongs engendered in a passion-distraught world 20 years
ago. I have inflicted enough vapourings on you for the
time! You can show this letter to anyone you like. It repre-
sents my firm convictions.

With fondest love, my dearest Bunt,
Ever your loving brother,
Tid

Vernede, the poet whom Uncle Tid quotes, was Robert Ernest Vernede, an English poet and writer. When war broke
out in 1914, though at 39 he was officially too old, Vernede
enlisted with the army as a second lieutenant in the 3rd Battalion Rifle Brigade. He served in France and was wounded
at the Battle of the Somme. Later, having refused a desk job,
he returned to the front, where he died while leading an advance at Havrincourt.

Though Vernede wrote a number of short stories and
novels, he is now best remembered as a war poet, one of
G. K. Chesterton's 'shining company of poets whose patri-
otism turned them into soldiers, and gave them a life and
death more worthy of legend'. That line – 'Peace... the
Peace which passeth understanding... Not in our time, but

in their time, O Lord' – was of course echoed by the most famous line in Prime Minister Chamberlain's declaration on his return from Munich on September 30th 1938, when he brandished the Anglo-German Naval Agreement, signed by Hitler, committing both nations to peace.

Standing outside 10 Downing Street, Chamberlain told the nation, 'My good friends, for the second time in our history, a British Prime Minister has returned from Germany bringing peace with honour. I believe it is peace for our time. We thank you from the bottom of our hearts. Go home and get a nice quiet sleep.'

Alas, 'Peace for our time,' was a hollow hope. How sad it is to know that Uncle Tid's wish, that we children as we were then, might still have a choice of a 'saner and more wholesome world', did not come to pass and that less than a year later, Britain and Germany were at war. Chamberlain's strategy of 'appeasement' with regard to Hitler's Germany had failed.

Uncle Tid served in WW2 of course, in the 8th Destroyer Flotilla. His ship, HMS Faulknor was the first destroyer to sink a German U-boat. In 1941, Uncle Tid became Captain of HMS Renown. He was made Flag Officer Combined Operations in 1943 and Vice Admiral in charge of administration for the British Pacific Fleet in 1944. After the war, he spent four years as Third Sea Lord and Controller of the Navy before becoming Commandant of the Imperial Defence College, a role he held until his retirement in 1952.

THE BOMBER WITH MORE THAN 50,000 PARTS: SKELETON VIEW OF A LANCASTER, WHICH LEADS THE WORLD IN ITS CLASS.

PART TWO

During the War

CHAPTER TWENTY-SIX

Pat

Among the Christmas presents I received in December 1938 was a 1939 diary from Aunt Gioia in which to write my impressions as we travelled through the year. Though it was to be a year which changed all our lives, my account of it begins rather unpromisingly.

> *Sunday January 1st... Not feeling at all New Year-ish. Burst Mummy's satin stays whole way down twice – I was wearing them. Must mug up Latin... Why do small things drive one to frenzies at night that never worry one a bit by day... Impressions so far very prosaic and uninteresting. Foresee that I shall spend nights trying to invent really good impressions. Originally meant to publish this some day. Now see il faut that I burn it!*

The early months of the year continue in a similar vein. I still disliked school as much as ever, complaining of 'dreary nights and drearier days'. I even tried to persuade my parents that I should be allowed to leave, to no avail. Though Jean doubtless hated being the only one of the three of us siblings still living at home, I was desperately envious of her having Newland and our mother all to herself. I found many of my classmates insufferable, I hated gym lessons and I loathed having to go to the 'smelly' baths at Leamington for swimming. I was a teenager of some passion when it came to the things I didn't want to do.

There were some brighter moments, however. At the beginning of the year, I was made a prefect, a role which came with a purple girdle – a belt – to wear with my school uniform and other privileges. I was enjoying my art lessons, and spent time drawing and painting whenever I was able.

There were pranks to be played, too. I was one of two girls hoping to take a school certificate in Latin. We were being prepared for the examination by Miss Jolly, otherwise known as 'The Bird'. Ahead of each class – I was having six Latin lessons a week – my classmate and I would scan through the set texts and pick one that we'd ask The Bird to read aloud for us. Naturally, we would try to find the rudest texts among the 45 we had been given to learn by heart.

'We'd like to do number 18, Miss Jolly,' we'd say, quite innocently, when she arrived.

Choosing something that started 'Oh Lesbia,' was a favourite ruse, guaranteed to have us stifling giggles while poor Miss Jolly blushed. After a while, she must have known what we were up to whenever we expressed enthusiasm for a certain piece.

In the sheltered confines of The Laurels, it would have been easy to ignore what was going on in the world outside, but I continued to keep up with the news.

In March 1939, I wrote:

Awful grave news about Czechoslovakia. It seems such a little time since September and now Hitler is trying to expand again. It is awful, living on the edge of this gulf. Hitler acting like utter swine. O how lovely life would be without this slimy dread of war always looming up. But how much worse to be a German Jew... Heard Chamberlain speak from Birmingham. Awfully impressed. Says he will give anything for peace but not Britain's freedom. Sounded very tired, but nice voice. Never sounds very grave and we go on living just the same...

Then for a while my attention went back to a hockey tournament and reading Margaret Mitchell's 'Gone With The Wind' which I found 'very rude in parts'. So rude, in fact, that my dormitory mates and I devoted most of our prep time to reading it.

In April, while I was home for the Easter holidays, Italy invaded Albania. The Albanian royal family, King Zog and Queen Geraldine and their eight-day old baby son Leka, went into exile, while Mussolini crowed about the expansion of the Italian empire and set a puppet king, Victor Emmanuel III, on the Albanian throne.

The news worried the adults.

Daddy quite anxious for war. I agree, this is very immoral. Grandboffin nestled round the radio all day in hope of news. He even listened to the daily service In order to hear the ten o'clock bulletin. Unheard of before... Italians have declared King Zog an outlaw. Damned cheek, it's his

country, not theirs. Am furious. Daddy expressed Easter-
like wish to murder Mussolini at lunch. I agree.

In solidarity with the Albanians, Bob christened his two
new guinea pigs Zog and Geraldine.

In the United States, President Roosevelt tried to put a
stop to this empire-building in Eastern Europe. He made a
speech on April 15th, demanding pledges from Germany
and Italy that they would not attack any foreign countries,
including Britain. I wrote, 'If it comes off, best thing for
some time. To last for $10 - 25$ years and conferences to be
held about disarmament and the news much cheerier. I
always did like Americans.' By now it seems I had forgiven
the 'beastly Americans' for Wallis Simpson.

The day after Roosevelt made his speech, something quite
amazing occurred. Two trumpets, one silver and one bronze,
which had been found in the tomb of the Egyptian boy king
Tutankhamun were played for the first time in millennia.
Some 150 million people tuned in to hear the trumpets on
an international broadcast by the BBC. Jean, Bob and I were
among them, listening in on Grandboffin's radio.

16th April 1939. Heard Tutankhamun's Trumpets on BBC
from Egypt. Weird noise. 3,000 years ago people heard
same sound across Egypt's sands. People I shall never know
names of. Longing to go to Egypt and Arabia.

The myth of the curse of Tutankhamun is well-known.

It's said that when bandsman James Tappern of Prince Albert's Own 11th Royal Hussars played the trumpets for the first time on that day in April 1939, the silver trumpet was shattered, causing Alfred Lucas, who had restored the instruments, such distress that he had to be taken to hospital to recover from the shock.

More recently, the unbroken bronze trumpet was stolen from Cairo's Egyptian Museum during the 2011 'Egyptian Revolution'. When the trumpet was returned to the museum several weeks later, a rumour went about that the trumpet had magical powers and that whenever it was sounded, a war would break out. Apparently, it had been blown immediately prior to the Gulf War of 1991 and before that, ahead of the Arab-Israeli 'Six Day War' of 1967. It's interesting to wonder now whether the BBC broadcast of the trumpets in 1939 had tempted fate?

Certainly, Hitler had not been put off by Roosevelt's speech on non-aggression pledges. On April 28th Hitler responded with a speech of his own, which began with a sarcastic reference to the fact that Roosevelt's message had been published all over the world before he'd had time to hear it.

'Hitler spoke for two hours and ten minutes,' I wrote on April 29th. 'Listened to all bulletins. Tho' I suppose he is such an ogre, it seems everyone who meets him simply adores him. I think Goebbels and Co are the fearable ones. Hitler's pretty ill. Could this have caused his conduct?'

I spent that night jumping up and down with a torch, worried by every creak and sigh the house made in the dark.

A couple of days later, I was back at school. Between war and exams there was so much to be worried about.

July 2nd 1939. Coventry Cathedral for evensong. Somehow duller than usual. Usually enjoy it very much but didn't this time. Must be due to general school certificate depression.

I had no idea on that day that I had seen inside that beautiful medieval cathedral for the last time, nor could I have guessed how the fate of Coventry and its people was intertwined with the events playing out in Berlin, Vienna and Rome.

I sat my exams as expected and the school year ended. I was very glad to be home for the summer, though I still hadn't persuaded my parents that I should not go back to The Laurels in September, when I would be joined there by Jean.

In mid-August, we took a family holiday in the West of Scotland. Our parents had borrowed a caravan from a neighbour and we were having a wonderful time. We were joined by our mother's cousin Monica. We paid our respects to Bonnie Prince Charlie at the Glenfinnan monument. Jean and I fished for trout at Loch Morar with our father, and were delighted to attend a local Highland Games, where I fell for the handsome young laird. We travelled over to Skye and saw the Northern Lights.

But those rumblings of war were getting louder again. We had pitched our camp on a farm and each evening we were invited into the farmhouse to hear the news. On August 24th, I wrote, 'Aunt Monica went back to do Red Cross work. It can only be war now.'

It wasn't long before our father decided that he needed to be with his regiment. We cut short our trip and returned to Newland, where we were met by Uncle Tom and Aunt Gioia and cousin Jill. A day later, Uncle Tom and Aunt Gioia decided that they should go back to London, leaving Jill with us for the time being. Everybody sensed that war was on the horizon but no-one knew how suddenly and dramatically it might start. It seemed only sensible to be ready for an immediate German attack.

29th August. News very grave... situation worsening. Germany looks like invading Poland...Thursday 31st Everything prepared for war... Everyone praying very half-heartedly for peace. All men look very set, but really revelling in it. We live clustered round the wireless, and everybody says 'How like 1914'. I feel very old and efficient.

On September 1st, Germany invaded Poland. I wrote, '"The lights go out over Europe". Is this the end of civilisation? We must declare war. We can't repeat the Munich let-down. Waiting – waiting – waiting.'

Just two days later, on September 3rd 1939, we gathered around the radio before church to hear Prime Minister Chamberlain make a speech to the nation, telling us that we were at war. 'War declared. Heard 11.15 speech in Gertie Brennand's cottage. Thank the lord, no more suspense'.

CHAPTER TWENTY-SEVEN

Jean

Pat might have felt some relief at the declaration on September 3rd 1939, but the outbreak of war left me in a terrible state of suspense.

The adults in our lives immediately made themselves useful. Our father began training with his regiment. Our mother was already an ARP (Air Raid Precautions) warden and had been apprised of what she would have to do in the event of an invasion. Uncle Tom was in the war office, dealing with anti-aircraft arrangements. Aunt Gioia joined the Fire Service, which seemed to attract a great many writers and artists.

My only fervent hope was that the war would not prevent me from being able to join Pat at boarding school. I was itching to be away from governesses and Newland Hall and had been looking forward to starting at The Laurels all summer. I was extremely relieved to hear that I would still be allowed to go. On September 26th, which Pat referred to in her diary as a 'miserable, loathly day', I joined her on the journey to Warwickshire for my very first term at boarding school.

I had prepared for this big adventure by reading all the boarding school books I could lay my hands on and I was very excited at the thought of the midnight feasts that lay ahead. Alas, I was quickly disabused of the idea that The Laurels was going to be anything like Enid Blyton's fictional Whyteleafe School.

All the same, I think perhaps I had a happier time at school than Pat did. Being good at games, rather than academic, possibly made it easier for me to make friends. And it was lovely to be at school with my big sister. Pat was my link with home – keeping me from feeling too melancholic about being away from Newland.

The war did change some things about that first term. One of the big pluses about The Laurels was that it was close to Stratford-Upon-Avon, but the theatre and other cultural outings that Pat had so enjoyed during her first two years at the school were no longer possible. Upon the declaration of war, the theatres had been closed. They would eventually reopen, but obviously the teachers at The Laurels had lost their appetite for taking groups of girls away from the safety of the school. Instead of theatre trips and other cultural excursions, we had gas mask drills. When the air raid warnings sounded, we would be ushered out into the grounds, away from the risk of falling masonry, or down into the cellars that were used for music practice (and smoking, when the teachers weren't around).

As we were two years apart, Pat and I didn't have much to do with each other during the school day but our paths sometimes crossed in our free time. Pat was a prefect, but I know that she disliked many of the duties that entailed. She especially disliked having to make an inspection of the dorms at lunchtime and report back which of the girls had not made their beds properly. To make Pat's life easier, I was always careful to make my bed and not to get up to anything rebellious in front of her. She and her fellow prefects seemed so grown up. They had their own common room. In a cupboard in that room was a skeleton on a stand that the prefects called 'Timothy'. It was rumoured that the skeleton was part ape and part human female. Whatever it was, it always made an appearance at Halloween.

Most weekday evenings, all the girls would gather in Miss Jolly's study to listen to her read while we knitted socks for soldiers. It was an opportunity for us to have a little fun with our teacher. Just as Pat tried to get Miss Jolly to read out the naughtiest verses in her Latin set texts, we would try to get 'the Bird' to inadvertently start reading something rude from the books in her room. What fun it was to see her getting flustered as she realised she was getting to a naughty bit. At the end of each evening, it was the responsibility of the girl sitting next to the Bird to give a vote of thanks. We called this duty 'laying an egg'.

A girls' school in the ruins of Wroxall Abbey was not an obvious target for the Luftwaffe but the German pilots often unloaded unused bombs over the Warwickshire country-side and that's exactly what happened on the night of the Coventry Blitz. We woke the following morning to find an unexploded parachute mine in the school grounds. At Bob's school nearby, the pupils dug their own raid-proof trenches, which he proudly showed us on a weekend visit. It was lovely to be close enough to Bob to have tea with him on a Sunday afternoon.

Pat often told me that her last day at school could not come quickly enough. As we drove away at the end of Pat's final term, Pat tells me that she thought to herself, 'Never in my life will I be as miserable again as I have been at this place.' But I was happy at The Laurels and to my mind there's no doubt that boarding school life prepared us both for the experience of working and living alongside other women in the service roles we did not yet know lay ahead.

CHAPTER TWENTY-EIGHT

Pat

Jean and I have written at length about our wartime experiences in the women's services in our first volume of memoir, 'Codebreaking Sisters'. It's typical that it wasn't until after finishing that book that we unearthed my diaries from 1940 and 1941 and a handful of previously forgotten letters also dating from that time. I hope you will indulge us as we reproduce some of those diary entries here and revisit our lives in the early years of WW2, before we both donned uniforms.

In the summer of 1940, I had left school but I was still too young to join up and so I was back at home in Lancashire, waiting for September to roll around, when I hoped to be going to London to take a course at secretarial college. Since Jean and I were quite young, our parents had prepared us for the fact that there was only enough money to put one of us three children through university and that would have to be Bob, our brother. Jean and I had the choice of secretarial college or finishing school. Disinterested in learning to cook cordon bleu, I chose secretarial college, hoping that at least I might pick up some skills that would be useful for a future career in journalism, but there were many months to go before I could leave for London.

Our father had rejoined his regiment as soon as war was

declared but for now they were still training nearby and we were able to see him quite often. He would come home whenever he could and we in turn were invited to visit him at the barracks where the 137th were based.

All around, the landscape had been subtly changing, as the nation prepared in earnest for the German invasion we all assumed was inevitable. Concrete gun-towers were popping up everywhere like big grey mushrooms. At nights, we could sometimes hear the sound of the 'ack-ack' guns in the distance; anti-aircraft guns designed to shoot straight up into the sky. 'Ack-Ack' was the WW2 RAF signalese for 'AA', but it had a rather good onomatopoeic ring to it too.

Though Newland Hall was in the middle of nowhere, we occasionally saw RAF and German planes fly overhead. Dressed in his militia uniform, Grandboffin had prepared us all for an airborne invasion. Alongside our mother, Edie and Lilly, I was taught how to handle a rook rifle, practising on targets in the azalea beds. Jean, much to her annoyance, wasn't given firearms training but was instructed that in the case of an invasion, her role was to spirit Bobby – the all-important son and heir – away to safety in the farmhouse, while the rest of us slowed the Germans down with our guns.

I followed the progress of the war on all fronts. Each day, I read my father's newspapers and listened to the daily reports on the radio as I tried to make sense of what was going on. I wrote summaries of the information I had gleaned in my diary before I went to bed at night, recording the grim toll of the German air-raids and wondering whether each development on the continent made a German invasion of Britain more or less likely.

By July 1940, I felt things were looking very bleak.

'The hash this world is in!' I wrote. 'The whole thing is so useless, so bungled. One sometimes wonders how there can ever be peace again, how everything can ever be sorted out again… masses of troops and airmen on the station (they have the free always-open buffet for the services there) and naval officers saying goodbye to their wives and sweethearts. All this, with a background of sandbags, gives very last war effect, only more air force grey naturally. Roads crawling with RAF drivers under instruction.'

The adults tried to keep home life as normal as possible. In January of that year, rationing had come into force, beginning with food.

Some items, such as meat, cheese and sugar, were directly rationed with specific coupons. Others, such as tinned goods and dried fruit, were rationed using a points-based system.

In the kitchen, Edie improvised marvellously, making gorgeous Viennese cakes, using dried fruit and nuts. Icing sugar and golden syrup were no longer available, so Edie used almond paste. Even Grandboffin had to admit that she worked miracles, even if her Austrian recipes weren't to his usual taste.

I was especially annoyed by the rationing of soap – you could only buy one bar at a time – and writing paper. Every scrap of paper was suddenly precious. I covered every page of my diaries, which were already very small, with tiny hand-writing, abbreviating sentences to fit the maximum number of thoughts on a page. The price of everything was going up and even though fruit and vegetables weren't rationed, unless you grew them yourself, which fortunately we did at Newland Hall, they were less easy to come by as the Germans targeted our commercial shipping.

Though he was living with his regiment, Daddy would occasionally be able to come to Newland Hall for tea. He regaled us with stories from his barracks, such as the time a sentry gave the alarm that parachutists were coming, sending the whole camp into a scramble, only to put on his glasses and realise that what he had actually seen was the top of one of the balloon barrages over the trees.

Our father's battery was now stationed in Knowsley Park, near Prescot. His regiment had been divided up and tasked with guarding aerodromes around Liverpool and Wales. Their camps were rudimentary but some batteries were faring better than others by 'borrowing' raw materials from the local people. Daddy told us about one battery that had become known as 'super-looters'. I recounted the story in my diary:

Their gun pits are floored with paving stones, concrete, marble chips and some very nice rounded kerbstones, all of which they have unscrupulously seized from their rightful owners. They needed paving stones, and a lorry was sent off with a raiding party. In the outskirts of Liverpool they saw some very nice large flat pavement stones, parked the lorry at the side of the street, and began pulling them up. A policeman came along and said, 'Hi, stop, what d'you think you're doing?' and the raider in charge replied, 'We've orders to build a blockhouse here, and we've got to pull all these up first. Lend us a hand, mate.' The bobby took his coat off and helped them put the stones into the lorry. They then drove away. No doubt he is still waiting hopefully for the blockhouse to be built.

Providing security for the aerodromes meant that the officers of the 137th were working closely with the RAF, who gave them reports from a bird's eye view.

One pilot told Major Lambert, when he called there a day or two ago, that during one day's flying over Cheshire he had counted 15 German aircraft, reconnoitring. There are masses more over all the time, he says, than anybody realises. They dropped bombs so near the RA HQ that all the windows were smashed, all but hit the railway line at Crewe and bombed Old Trafford. They haven't dropped many bombs on L'Pool. A few in the Mersey. Also they attempted to lay mines in it. Daddy says they are woken up often by AA gunfire six miles away and he has heard explosions from bombs and falling aircraft. He is thoroughly enjoying the life...

It wasn't only our father who was seeing and hearing the action close by.

On Wednesday July 31st, 1940, I wrote:

Fastest plane I've seen lately has just gone hurtling by.

Such amazing speed. Heysham was casually bombed last night. Mummy saw a brilliant flash of light followed by an explosion at about 1am today, sat up, thought it was probably lightning, and went to sleep again. We heard at Burgesses in Galgate, however, that it was Morecambe and Heysham. Golf course bombed, clubhouse windows blown in. Mrs Redmayne from Bailrigg had heard several bombs, house shaken. Bosch plane had been over Galgate. M heard it...

...Aunt Ellie says that Aunt Ella called and said she had so much enjoyed being bombed, and had gone out for a walk during an air raid. Foolhardy, no doubt: wish Hitler could hear of this curious outlook of the British maiden lady.

...11.40pm, aeroplane just gone over towards NW, low and with no lights. Galgate police think it was German – our planes apparently show lights when over England. Saw two today with white markings, possibly German cross, but could only see that it was not British tricolour circle. Seems unlikely that they could sail over with no AA or fighter opposition.

Ten months into the war, it was perhaps understandable that some people weren't feeling as gung-ho as they had been in September 1939.

To gauge public support, the Ministry of Information, led by Duff Cooper, decided they needed to gather some vox pop. Sixty people were employed, under the auspices of the

National Institute for Economics and Scientific Research, to go house to house asking for opinions. The initiative did not go down well. I certainly found it ridiculous. It smacked of the sort of surveillance one might expect in Hitler's Germany.

Much feeling, especially in the Daily Mail, against the "Duff-Snoopers" – system instituted by Ministry Of Information of sending inquisition callers to many homes (calling themselves Mr and Mrs Sensible) to ask the harassed housewife "Are You Downhearted?" As they specialise in visiting pubs, the answers they get (as the Church Times points out) are probably not representative of the British Public. Whole idea savours of the Gestapo, is quite unnecessary. Good cover for spies to call and ask questions helpful to the enemy and revolting waste of money in wartime. – £1,000 a month, which would be better spent in Defence Bonds...

Many in the House of Commons agreed with me. As did the Chief Constable of Derby, 'It is a lot of silly nonsense... We all have quite enough to do without this.' I think he spoke for all of us.

CHAPTER TWENTY-NINE

Pat

At the beginning of August, with Jean and Bob home from school, our mother drove us to visit Daddy at his camp in Knowsley. The troops were to be inspected by Lord Derby, who owned the estate upon which the camp had been set up. It was the first time we'd really got to see where our father was living and working. It was an interesting day, where we saw the good and the bad of army life. Home again in the evening, I wrote this account, which gives a flavour of how the war had changed the landscape of all our lives.

Sunday, August 4th, 1940.

Just back from Knowsley. Nice day, hazy and warm. Started at 9am for Liverpool, Mummy, Jean, Robert and I in the car. Went rather out of our way to Aintree, as M hadn't brought Daddy's instructions. Roads very well prepared, innumerable blocks each with concrete blockhouse and barbed-wire entanglement. Very good one just beyond Preston, and in outskirts of Liverpool. Passed several camps – one for enemy male aliens; and many wounded soldiers in hospital uniform. All tents, hangers etc and many cars camouflaged. All services much in evidence.

Reached Knowsley Church during Te Deum. Just in time to hear Daddy read second lesson.... Entire regiment minus "fancy religions" and absent batteries in church, sung "Praise the Lord ye Heavens adore him" and "Oh God our help" very well – raised the roof.

...Afterwards talked to Mrs Hale – Christian name Queen, wife of George (there was once apparently much excitement in country village where friends of theirs live, when Post Office received following telegram: "Arrive tomorrow, George and Queen"). Lord Derby then inspected troops, asked one about his war ribbons, spoke a few words, and troops marched off. We followed by car to camp....

Went round most of the camp with the Colonel, Mrs Garland and one Belfield, a subaltern, who monopolised – or was monopolised – by me. Saw cookhouses – very unhygienic, though one does not say so – with incredibly Heath Robinson arrangement of troughs, boxes, corrugated iron and sink pit, to get rid of washing up water. Belfield told me that each man washes his own plate up, which saves kitchen maids and can be adapted to individual taste – some wash carefully and often, others never.

Met small car racing down cinder road at about 15mph, which was stopped by Col. and reminded that speed limit in camp is five mph. Then inspected transport – lorries, vans, cars of every description and stage of disintegration. I remarked that it looked like motor-show at Olympia, which showed considerable tact, but, as the Col. pointed out, was rather an insult to Olympia.

Then visited 45 Howitzers. Also ammunition for same.

Shell and charge are separate. Shell is rammed in first, then charge, which is adjustable, and gun is then fired. Also saw very big consignment of shells for French 75 gun, just come from America. This is some of last-war stock they have sent over – shells made 1918, filled and packed 1919... very long and carefully packed in tin bands, brown paper etc, weighed about 12 lb each – and rattled in a most extraordinary way, as if charge in each had become loose through keeping. Everyone rather flabbergasted by this. They hope to get a number of French 75s from US soon. These shells useless to them at present as they do not fit 45 Howitzers (shells for these cost about £3 each, plus charge).

Men's tents are pitched all down both side of avenue, like a street of wigwams. At the end are the officers' tents and mess on the left going down, cook and store-houses and men's mess tents on right, gas-detectors and gateway straight on.

We drove up the avenue – Daddy having changed from 'rompers and a side hat' into posher rig – and had lunch on the north side of Knowsley Lake, which looked very like a loch with bracken and islands etc. Excellent picnic lunch – Edie had cut dozens of tomato sandwiches, and continuous roar of tanks in the background.

After lunch... Followed track through park to corner occupied by Tank Regiment, who were all over the place in black berets. Daddy knows their C.O, 2nd in Command, adjutant etc and found a very nice subaltern called Jones who came with us to small wood surrounded by RTR's (Royal Tank Regiment) transport – bread vans, pantech-

nicons etc, very assorted. Then found that eight or nine tanks were parked under trees, heavy tanks, mediums and babies. We were joined by nice and good-looking friend of Mr Jones's wearing black beret: a captain, addressed as "Pim". Both full of information and enthusiasm, and enlarged on agony of being inside a tank.

We all climbed all over and into a baby one, very very little space inside, once in, in for good, hellishly hot (they say) and dark, and smelly!!!

Driver sits downstairs, getting in either by back or front door. He can then see nothing, and drives tank by levers which control one side each. Tank Commander gets in thro' turret and sits facing the other way and directs driver through speaking tube. If the driver can't, as usual, hear, TC kicks him on shoulder, right or left, according to which way he wants to go. TC keeps his forehead glued to leather pad on periscope, which he swivels round when he wants to see the other way. He sits facing a dashboard covered with dials and switches. Beside him is a long belt of machine gun ammunition, in a box – many more boxes in floor.

All over the inside are electric light switches, and there is an electric fan – both very necessary. Roof of turret is padded, as progress of tank is bump-bump-bump action. Number three climbs in and works machine-gun. Whole turret swivels round by means of internal lever – 'Pim' performed this for us. TC also works wireless –wireless mast cannot be snapped by branches etc as it is fixed on so as to bend in any direction.

Can imagine nothing more uncomfortable and impos-

sible to fight in, and am not surprised at large number of Russians found dead in their tanks last winter in Finnish war. "Churchill," said Lt Jones, "has always taken a keen interest in tanks and done a lot to encourage use of them."

"Pim" and Mr Jones have been at Speke Aerodrome for some time (Q. What advantage can flying experience be to tank officers?) and have also been doing aerial photography... Left Tanks, who have a very nice flag flying by fire alarm etc at their gate, and proceeded to Aerodrome, but were not allowed inside, and no planes going up. Then on via Cathedral – very fine – to Mersey Tunnel, with which I was delighted to renew acquaintance, and Jean and Bob, for whom it was the first time, were thrilled. Through and back again. One has to show one's identity card at each end. At both mouths are rows of ancient cars to make a bloc, squares full of barbed wire.

Back to mess for tea...Then home, via rather minor roads, where French sailors in rather attractive red caps were flirting with local lasses, to main road at Old Ram Inn. Picked up soldier laddie, who wanted a lift at Ormskirk, and dropped him at church town corner. Arrived home about 7.15pm.

CHAPTER THIRTY

Jean

Every evening we tuned in the radio to listen to the news. There was more than enough bad news but there were stories to boost our morale too, and reports of traitors unveiled.

On Thursday 9th August, 1940, Pat wrote in her diary, 'most thrilling account of escape and adventures of three Highlanders in France given by man from Ballachulish on the wireless today. On second capture they spoke Gaelic continuously and convinced Germans that they came from Ukraine. Eventually escaped to Spain…'

Like Pat, I was fascinated by the story of the soldiers who had conned the Germans with such style. It was absolutely true. The three men in question were Private William Kemp, Corporal Sandy MacDonald and Lance Corporal James 'Ginger' Wilson of the Argyll and Sutherland Highlanders.

After their regiment surrendered to the Germans, the brave trio managed to escape and swapped their uniforms for civilian clothes but were quickly recaptured at a checkpoint. Taken to a prisoner of war camp, they were brought before the German camp commander who pointed his revolver at each of the men in turn, in an attempt to intimidate them into talking. A French officer, acting as interpreter, asked the men to state their nationality. Thinking quickly, the first of the men replied in Gaelic, claiming not to understand the question. The others followed suit. They kept up this pretence while being questioned in seven more languages. Finally Private Kemp gave the name of his town, 'Ardnamurchan', which was sufficiently strange-sounding to the French interpreter and the German guards to convince them that the men in front of them were in fact speaking Ukrainian. Since Ukraine was not at that point at war with Germany, the three were subsequently released and travelled through occupied France to Spain, presenting themselves at a British consulate there. From Spain they were returned by ship to Scotland.

The daring escape had a happy ending for the three quick-witted soldiers, but when the Germans realised how they had been duped, they retaliated by sending any captives known to speak Gaelic to a labour camp. The Germans were showing every day how ruthless they could be and at home in England, we felt we were part of a waiting game.

At around the same time, we heard about the unveiling of 'Lord Haw Haw'.

Haw-Haw was the nickname of William Brooke Joyce, an American-born fascist and Nazi propaganda broadcaster. Joyce was born in New York, to an Irish father and a mother from Lancashire. When he was a young boy, the family returned to Galway in Ireland.

During the Irish War of Independence, Joyce found himself acting as a courier for the British Army. After the partition of Ireland, the Joyce family moved back to England, to avoid retribution. Young William joined the Worcestershire Regiment, but it was discovered that he was underage and he was subsequently discharged.

After gaining a first-class degree in English from Birkbeck College, in London, Joyce applied to join the Foreign Office. After he was rejected, he worked as a teacher. It was about this time that he became interested in Fascism, associating with the British Fascists.

In 1932, Joyce joined Oswald Mosley's British Union of Fascists and was quickly promoted to the position of the BUF's Director of Propaganda. He led the party's decision to focus on antisemitism and pushed for the name change to the 'British Union of Fascists and National Socialists' to bring it in line with the National Socialists in Germany. He was known as a powerful speaker and a brawler. He claimed that the scar that ran across his face was the result of a razor slash delivered by a Jewish attacker. His first wife is believed to have dismantled that particular fiction, saying his attacker was in fact an Irish woman.

Joyce left England for Berlin shortly before the outbreak of war, having been warned that as soon as war was declared, he would be detained by the British authorities. There he became a German citizen and took a job reading the news in English on German radio. He soon became a Nazi propagandist, broadcasting first from Berlin and then Hamburg, and writing 'black propaganda' scripts for the German 'Buro Concordia', which pretended to be broadcasting from within Britain. He wrote propaganda leaflets intended to encourage British POWs to join the British Free Corps of the Waffen-

SS. He lectured on British Fascism at the University of Berlin.

Joyce got his name 'Lord Haw Haw', after Jonah Barrington, a British newspaper radio critic who described hearing a man on German radio moaning in 'English of the haw-haw-damit-get-out-of-my-way variety'. It was not illegal for people living in the United Kingdom to listen to Lord Haw Haw's broadcasts and it's believed that as many as 18 million people tuned in to hear him talk, perhaps keen to know how the Germans thought the war was going on at their end. He opened each broadcast in the same way, saying, 'Germany calling, Germany calling.'

Joyce was unveiled as Lord Haw Haw in August 1940. Pat wrote about the moment in her diary.

Very interesting recording on news last night by American news-man who has spent last year or so in Berlin. He was one of four who broadcast in English the news, as part of a news-chain, from Berlin. They had the same conditions as foreign correspondents, except that they were censored. He said that Lord Haw Haw (Englishman called Joyce) used to go on just before him. There were several Englishmen in the studio, one had an English mother. All talked very bad German in front of the Americans. On the night that Joyce's identity was revealed in London, he asked someone else to read the news for him. It's an awful dirty job, I think.

Joyce made his last broadcast in April 1945, during the Battle of Berlin, signing off 'Heil Hitler and Farewell'. He was captured by British forces a month later and identified by a Jewish intelligence officer who recognized his voice. When Joyce reacted to the question of his identity by reaching into his pocket, his captors assumed he was retrieving a hidden weapon and shot him in the buttocks.

Tried on three counts of high treason at the Old Bailey, Joyce was eventually sentenced to be hanged. He died at Wandsworth Prison in 1946, the last but one person to be executed for treason in the United Kingdom. He was unrepentant to the end, making an antisemitic speech even as he went to his death, adding 'I am proud to die for my ideals.'

CHAPTER THIRTY-ONE

Pat

The popularity – for whatever reason – of Lord Haw Haw was problematic. It was important to keep public morale high. At the same time, it also felt important to maintain a sense of national identity and for me, that meant not succumbing to the temptation to stoop to the kind of cruelty of which Hitler's followers had shown themselves capable.

While I was at home, I helped our mother with her Mother's Union duties and went with her to meetings in Lancaster to listen to speakers sent by the Ministry of Information, which had made me so angry with its 'Duff Snoopers'. One such meeting shows how the war was dividing public opinion.

Tuesday, August 13th, 1940. In the afternoon we went to a Women's Meeting in Lancaster... Speaker – very good indeed – was Professor Ramsey Muir. All very patriotic – platform draped with Union Jacks, rows of Representative Women. Most atrocious black-beetle called Councillor Hurst followed with the most appalling speech I've ever heard. Very poor delivery, and he went on and on and on about how he was the one who would soon be fighting to protect us, how he had two kiddies, one six, the other four, and he knew that if anything happened to them he knew there were no lengths to which he would not go to revenge them, there must be no mercifulness in this war etc etc etc, and kept saying that he spoke for all of us which was far from being the case. Whole thing was pure distilled jingoism.

Well, at last he sat down, and Aunt Flo (who was charming and very popular in the chair) called on tall officer called Capt. Radcliffe to propose a vote of thanks. Such a relief to hear crisp military speech after awful derailing sob stuff of Councillor Hurst (should be spelt 'Hearsed') and he did his stuff very nicely about Aunt Flo and the Professor, and then came to Hurst, giving the main points of his speech much more clarity than Hurst had done, and said that on one point he would like to cross swords with him. Rather than see the women of England urging on airmen to bomb the women and children of Germany (which is what Hurst wanted) he would see England go down, he said. I was entirely in agreement. He then remarked – "Rather long speech I'm afraid – hope you'll show appreciation in the usual manner" – and sat down.

Sir Launcelot Sanderson rose to second the vote (I like his gentlemanly bloodhound face). Spoke pretty about Aunt Flo and Professor, and touched on Hurst, who was now generally unpopular.

Aunt Flo acknowledged all compliments very nicely, ditto Professor, and Mr Hurst said that although he and Captain R had different views on one subject, he would show British chivalry from further argument to which Capt. R had no chance of replying… He spoiled a meeting at which the

whole atmosphere was completely harmonious and sensible
– odious slush-sloshing creature.

We were still expecting an invasion. In the summer of 1940, Paris had fallen to the Nazis. We'd seen the miraculous but humiliating evacuation from Dunkirk. The Battle of Britain was raging above our heads.

On Wednesday, August 14th, I wrote:

Goering threatens next weekend will be a bad one for England – nothing he has done so far is faintly comparable with what he will do this weekend. Mme Tabouis foretold this invasion for between Aug 15th – 20th – the day on which Hitler said he would dictate peace terms from London. Just heard – 88 German planes brought down today, 19 of ours lost, five pilots saved. Yesterday, 31 Germans, seven or ours, of which two pilots returned. Also, the Germans attacked Croydon today, results not yet known.

RAF been damaging N. France and Germany as usual, four missing. Three of our planes patrolling met 24 returning Heinkels over Germany today, and brought down at least two with no loss to themselves. Have heard nothing from Japan for ages, nor about parachutes found in Midlands and Scotland. Edie is sure they brought down spies, possibly of English nationality, not soldiers. This I think is most probable, as they have probably brought instructions about the invasion, and are sent on ahead to prepare for it. Other alternative is that they are empty ones, dropped to

cause panic: but would they be heavy enough to open and
drop. Just been announced that second theory is correct.

Madame Tabouis was Genevieve Tabouis, a French histo-
rian and journalist who had repeatedly warned about the
rise of Hitler in the early '30s. Week after week, Tabouis
wrote columns for French newspaper *L'Oeuvre* that dissected
Hitler's political actions and even anticipated his next moves
in ways that disrupted his ability to carry them out. Tabouis
was rewarded for her efforts with unkind comparisons to
Cassandra, the mythical Trojan priestess cursed by Apollo to
have the gift of prophecy but never to have her predictions
and warnings believed. Hitler himself said that 'Madame
Tabouis knew yesterday what I am now saying to you at a
time I didn't know myself what I would say. But she knew
it, this wisest of all women.' He presented this as a joke but
Tabouis was so often right, that it's said that Hitler began to
believe she might actually be able to read his mind.

Tabouis had been right about Hitler's plans for Poland,
the Netherlands, Denmark, Norway and France. She fled
France for England in 1940, just before the French surrender
to Germany, having heard that a warrant had been issued for
her arrest.

She subsequently ended up in New York, where she edited
the French-language paper *Pour La Victoire* and wrote for
Sunday Dispatch, which was published out of London. That's
where I read her columns. Was she about to be proved right
again?

Our Air Chief Marshal, Sir Philip Bennet Joubert de la

Ferté reassured the nation that the RAF was doing its best to wreck Madame Tabouis' predictive record.

Saturday, August 18th, 1940, 7.05 pm. Rather hectic day... Our air-scores continue to amaze us and the world. 180 on Thursday – peak-day so far: yesterday 75, I think. We lost 22 – 14 pilots home. Joubert said on Thursday that people were beginning to say, Oh but there must be some mistake, we can't be doing so well really! "Our air-scores," he said, "are very carefully checked: we've spent a great deal of money and care on our Air Force and it's going like a hot knife through butter." Every enemy plane that raided Croydon was brought down, ditto with a party of dive-bombers that were attacking a south east aerodrome. SW London was also raided, and all the sirens in London sounded. The Ministry Of Information is letting out a lot more names of towns and counties raided.

...One nice story was told on the news about Aug 15. Just after Hitler had announced that he would be in London by that day, the Overseas League arranged to hold a meeting on Aug 15 and at the meeting two chairs were left empty, labelled "Hitler" and "Mussolini", as Lord Withingdon was making the opening speech, a telegram was handed to him, 'purporting to come from "The summerhouse, Berchtesgaden". It read – "Regret unable to attend meeting. Started according to plan but was blown back by a Hurricane. Adolf Hitler."

We are childish.

Another rather nice touch was when a patrolling British

plane saw a Heinkel seaplane lying on the water one night recently. It was an easy prey, but the British pilot was too sporting to shoot a sitting bird, so he dived towards it with his headlights on, and the Heinkel accepted the challenge and rose to the fight. A few minutes later it was in the water again, but this time ablaze. The British plane continued its patrol.

Not a single air raid today. Hope this won't inspire a false sense of entire, complacent confidence, specially in people like Grandboffin, who says that Hitler knows himself beaten, which, though the air battles may have tipped the balance, he certainly isn't yet. During the week, Germany lost 490 planes, Britain something over 100, between 1/4 and 1/3 a good many of our pilots safe, whenever they try to rescue German ones, they sink our boats. Duff Cooper spoke after the news: usual melancholy bombast.

Our father was still in Knowsley at this point and was still sometimes able to come and visit, as he did one August Sunday. It was wonderful to have him at home, to talk about what was happening in the war and other, lighter, things.

Sunday August 19th, 1940. At tea, Bobby remarked casually – Daddy having said he had had tea with two countesses and an earl during the week – 's'matter of fact, the headmaster and I had rather an amusing conversation one day last term.' – 'What did you talk about?' I asked. – "Oh well," said Bob. "He asked me what I fed my rabbits on."

...The Hardys, Mrs and David, wife and son of the outsize CO of Bowerham Barracks, came to tea for the first time.

"Well," said Bob to David, by way of pleasantry, "And how many soldiers died of fright when they thought there was going to be a war?"

Cheerful day, chiefly. I think, owing to relaxation of last week's tension. Not so much activity as before today – was disgusted by article in paper condemning forcibly action of British pilot in not attacking sitting Heinkel. It's exactly the attitude of not shooting the sitting bird which we are fighting for, and we shall do no good to our own cause by using the filthy weapons of the enemy.

Anyway, our pilots don't need to attack sitting birds – they are well capable of destroying ones in the air.

CHAPTER THIRTY-TWO

Pat

Though the Battle of Britain dominated the news, I still hoped that in September I would be heading to London to start that course at Ransom's Secretarial College. Thus I was extremely disappointed when my parents received a letter from Miss Ransom, proprietor, telling them that a lack of students necessitated the closing down of the college. It seemed that not everyone was as excited about the prospect of living in London in the middle of a war as I was.

Miss Ransom suggested a compromise. She could arrange for me to go on scholarship to The Triangle, a similar secretarial school where I could learn typing, shorthand, French, German and journalism. The Triangle didn't look as interesting as Ransom's but it still offered me a chance to leave home.

They had a branch in Gerrards Cross, on the edge of London, and another at Angmering On Sea, which would ordinarily have seemed quite safe but with the prospect of the Germans landing on the coast was perhaps even less safe than London. My parents agreed that it was best I stick to my London plans.

On the day Miss Ransom's letter arrived, Russian revolutionary Leon Trotsky was assassinated with an ice axe in

Mexico. I wrote in exasperation, 'All the interesting people will be dead before I'm interesting enough to be introduced to them.' Just a week later, the Germans tried an assassination too.

Wednesday August 29th. Daddy came home at 10.30pm with a large jagged triangle, part of a German shell, which had landed about 300 yds from his tent during the preceding night. As it was a screaming one, he was rather scared. The Bosch planes were very active during the night, as the King and Queen were known to be on a tour of the north-west. Lord Derby said he thought the Bosch were betting on them being at Knowsley for the night, which is why they dropped bombs at Croxteth, by Daddy's camp, and in the avenue of little trees leading to the houses. Actually Their Majesties were peacefully asleep in the royal train at Garstang siding.

There followed a whole week of raids on the north-west. We saw a good deal of AA barrage. 'Lovely bursts of golden fire all over the sky, and no sound at all,' is how I described them. 'As soon as the sirens go, we rush out into the garden to watch.'

It seemed that Lancashire was suddenly as dangerous as London but there was worse news on that front. Aunt Ellie wrote to my parents to tell them that she did not think it would be a good idea for me to be in London, while there were so many night raids.

The second week of September was particularly bad.

Saturday, September 7th 1940, 11.40 pm. I missed the nine o'clock news tonight, as I was talking to Lilly. But the others report that the biggest air battle of the war is going on over London – started at 5pm – the Germans sending over hundreds of bombers: – and Aunt Gioia, Grandbof-fin and I are waiting up for the midnight news. I should think This Is It. Hitler always chooses a Saturday. Our fighters are beyond praise, but I do wish it was over Dover or somewhere – not London.

…Wireless has just pipped. Raids on London are terrific. 21 German planes brought down, five of our fighters lost. Communique arrived, saying German total 65, ours 18, two pilots safe. German planes coming in from SE meeting those going back. Deutschland-sender staged a running commentary on the London raid, in which he said the German planes were making "great sacrifices". Rather spoilt by ending, which was warning to German people to take cover at the sound of sirens…

Wednesday September 11th, 1940. Churchill spoke on the six o'clock news awfully well, as usual. German shipping is massing from Norway to Biscay for the invasion, which must be soon, as the RAF bomb their barge concentrations every night, and the weather may break. Next week, said the Premier, may be one of the most vital in our history. Present time is comparable to the coming of the Spanish Armada and the days of Napoleon, but much more is at stake. The London raids are also part of the invasion scheme, to harass and distract the Government. In this they have failed. Also the Germans must have air supremacy for the invasion, which they haven't.

Thursday, 11.15pm. All-clear just gone after half-hour's alarm, during which I had a bath. Jean leant out of the window, and M put on her navy-blue slacks, got the warning (red) and waited. We had two alarms while Daddy was here, and lots of Ack-ack, but none since. They have been too busy with London. But each night the damage they do seems to decrease, though their incendiaries are no joke. So far they got one wing of Buck house, two newspaper offices, several hospitals and maternity homes, Mme Tussauds, and also St Paul's twice. Also Uncle Godfrey's office, of which yesterday's Times had a photo...

Friday. Altogether there were three warnings here last night. I heard masses of aircraft – or dreamt I did. A letter takes six or seven days now to come from London, a telegram 24 hours at the shortest to reach London.

Saturday September 14th, 1940. Got a letter from dear Edie (Krochmalnik). She spends the whole of every night in a shelter – like the rest of London – and sleeps very well. Letter was in German... Edie is very very brave.

Also heard from Miss Jenkins of The Triangle; Gerrards Cross seems safe enough. Yet another jittery letter from Aunt Ellie to Mummy, saying that she remade her will during one night's raid, went out one night and saw a huge red glow over the city and white light where the gas main was burning, also mysterious flashes from flares; was just missed by several bombs, next-door house windows smashed by shrapnel, and nearly every house in the district either gutted by fire, de-glassed or smashed in, one gathers. She seems to be in a much worse state of nerves than anyone else in London.

Personally, I think she exaggerates to M because she doesn't want the responsibility of having me anywhere near London, because she keeps saying 'Don't send her to Gerrards Cross, I know they say it's quite safe but there is a big aerodrome there, etc.' Her milkman rather amused her by saying how his daughter-in-law had hysterics when a bomb passed right through her house. "She didn't oughta carry on like that!" he remarked gravely. Oh I wish Hitler would either try his blighted invasion and get it over, or else drop it for the moment and do a bit of 'couping' in the Balkans...

Germans yesterday made a deliberate attack on Buckingham Palace. I think it shows some courage, actually, to drive through London's balloon barrage in daylight and bomb BP. But rather mis-directed courage. King and Queen are all right, but chapel and Quadrangle are smashed up. United States and us are very much annoyed.

Sunday September 15th, 1940, 9.30pm. On the nine o'clock it was reported that our fighters had brought down 165 (later 188) enemy planes during today, losing only 30 of ours, with ten pilots safe (25 of ours lost and 12 pilots safe). All over London and the SE. One German pilot who *bailed out was captured by soldiers, and a crowd rushed to seize bits of his parachute as souvenirs. A Hurricane pilot brought down three German bombers – watched by crowds – and was then shot down himself. He bailed out and landed in an awful temper at having been shot down and out of the fight... Yet another attack on Buckingham Palace, which smashed up the Queen's rooms but hurt no-one... They have removed the delayed action bomb from near St Paul's. Gosh, the bomb squad deserve VCs!*

If the bombing of Buckingham Palace was designed to shock Britain into a state of paralysis, it had the opposite effect. Despite advice to leave the city, the Royal Family had stayed in London and in the days after the palace was hit, the King and Queen visited the East End, where the Queen uttered one of her most famous lines, 'I am glad we have been bombed. Now we can look the East End in the eye.' It was a show of solidarity that meant a great deal to Blitzed Britain, showing as it did that we were all in it together.

The north of England was suffering bombing raids too. As I reported in my diary on September 14th:

Daddy was sent on a two mile detour when driving from L'Pool to Chester, because a delayed action aerial torpedo or something (aimed for Cammell Laird's but missed) had been embedded by the road for five days, without exploding... They have a good many raids on L'pool – a specially big one last Wednesday, but not much since. AA fire usually begins c. 10.15pm, and if it is just overhead, the regiment puts on its tin-hats. He told a rather nice story about his driver – a Lancashire lad.

Driver: Ah 'ad to walk 'ome for me leave last week, Major Cary, wi' me full equipment. There were an air-raid goin' on all the time.
Daddy: That must have been trying for you.
Driver: Nay, it didn't bother me mooch. Ah joost got a bit o' broken glass on me 'ead. Ah were passin' a 'ouse as was stroock an' the windows were blown out on to me tin 'at (he produced a scratched tin hat).
D: Did you see the bombs?
Driver: Ah, ah saw a lot o' them incendiaries. In fact, Ah put three aht meself as ah was goin' along. (All this in a day's work: he hadn't mentioned it to anybody.)

10.40 Daddy just gone... Today's newspapers say tomorrow will be Der Tag: tide right, moon right, weather right. Some bright soul suggesting that oil should be poured outside the Channel ports on the troubled waters and set alight. I don't see why the idea should be impracticable, but I suppose, like all intelligent suggestions, nobody regards it as their business to follow it up. Possibly our, today's, air success may deter the enemy: also our devastating bombing of their key points, which our planes carried out in appalling weather conditions, only one failing to return...

There was still no invasion but September 17th saw one of the biggest tragedies of the war unfold on the Atlantic.

While the Germans targeted British cities, it had been decided that it would be a good idea to evacuate as many children as possible to safer friendly countries including Canada, South Africa, New Zealand and the United States. The Children's Overseas Reception Board was formed to oversee the process. Shipping company Ellerman Lines donated three of their liners for the evacuation.

One of those liners was the SS City Of Benares. On September 13th 1940, City of Benares left Liverpool with 90 CORB evacuee children on board. Also onboard were ten other children, whose passage had been organised by their families. Benares joined a convoy, bound for Montreal. Halfway across the Atlantic, more than 600 miles from the nearest inhabited landmass, Benares was sighted by a U-boat and torpedoed. The captain ordered 'abandon ship' but only two of the 12 available lifeboats were successfully launched. One of them, containing six CORB children, was adrift at sea for eight days before its passengers were rescued. In the end, only 19 of the 100 children who had been onboard the Benares were saved.

The incident was a huge shock to public morale and saw the end of the policy of sending evacuees overseas. I wrote, before the final casualty numbers were released:

Tuesday, September 24th 1940. The King spoke very well indeed on the wireless at six o'clock last night. He was speaking from a shelter under the Palace, and one could hear the All-clear going just after he had begun. He spoke much less hesitantly than usual, and I think that his spaced words make his speeches more impressive. He announced the new decoration he has instituted – the George Cross, which is a civilian VC, and the George Medal for wider distribution.

Very cheering speech, just what the country was wanting. He praised everyone and expressed sympathy with the parents of the drowned children (whose evacuation ship, it was announced today, was sunk last Tuesday by a U-Boat, in a storm, and 600 miles from land. Seven of the 90 children were saved, two of their escorts. I forgot how many other passengers.). The King said it was yet another proof of the things we are fighting against...

CHAPTER THIRTY-THREE

Pat

Despite my fears, and the intensification of air raids, I was allowed to go to London to secretarial college after all. Well, not quite London. Gerrards Cross was where I would be staying. Still, it was close to the capital and that was good enough for me. I thought I knew London well, having spent so much time there, visiting Uncle Tom and Aunt Gioia in the school holidays, but the city was much changed since those days when Cousin Jill and I played hide and seek in Harrods. I recorded my impressions in November 1940.

Present address, the Triangle Secretarial College. I have been here nine weeks tomorrow. I travelled down by myself on Sat (Sept 22, I think) to Euston. I travelled with a very nice engineer who was going to see what had happened to his parents, their house having been bombed: and with an RAF man, who had been a driver for one of the road transport companies.

As we approached London, the train began to go very slow and kept stopping. We passed a large crater close to the line, and at one stop the guard came along shouting, "Shut your ventilators!" which means an air-raid. He told us the train was often three hours later, which was a bit

*annoying, as my train out to Gerrards Cross left Padding-
ton an hour after we should have reached Euston. However,
we reached London about 3/4 hour late and I got a taxi.*

*Wartime London is so different. There was an air raid
on, though no sign of it, and everyone walking about tired-
eyed but cheerful. We drove down Marylebone Road, same
crush of taxis and cars progressing in spurts, with exca-
vations (trenches and unexploded) along the roadside. I
looked down Tottenham Court Road, and saw the other
end was down. No glass in the Baker Street Tube Station
and the front of Mme Tussaud's much scarred. I kept seeing
horrors to right and left, the end of a building turned into
an avalanche of rubble: a gutted building, lovely regency
houses with no roofs or windows. You look at a row of
houses that is quite normal, and suddenly notice that half
of them have no window-glass.*

*We got to Paddington with the all-clear going, and
they said there were no trains going to Gerrards Cross
try Marylebone. So I re-embarked in my taxi, and when
we reached Marylebone the policeman said there were no
trains running from there at all, nor had been for a week
(when it had been bombed) and the only thing to do was
to go by underground from Baker Street to Wembley, and
change there into a bus to Wembley Hill, there by another
train to Gerrards X.*

*So I eventually arrived. We had an unexploded, and
two HEs which I heard fall about half a mile away, soon
after blackout. They screamed and cracked the glass of my
bedroom. We slept in a ground floor passage – very cold,*

hard and draughty – trailing upstairs when the all-clear went, or at 7am if it hadn't, for the first week I was there. I had a bedroom to myself, but when it became imminent that I would be moved into the dormitory (formerly the billiard room, 'sleeping' 8) owing to increasing congestion, I volunteered to evacuate to 'Calman', (much nicer). Rest of the term rather tedious. Spent weekends at Windsor, in town (with Edie etc). Home for two weeks for Xmas.

I didn't let my parents know about the excitement of my first night at the college, when the glass in my bedroom window was shattered by the HE bombs which were 'high explosive' bombs ranging between 50 and 500 kg in weight. They could cause a great deal of damage, not least because some of them were designed not to detonate on impact, but had timing mechanisms which might mean they exploded three days later, when nobody was expecting it. Aunt Ellie had been right. Gerrards Cross was perhaps not entirely safe.

But I survived my first term at The Triangle school and was glad to be in the south as just after Christmas, my father's regiment had been sent to Salisbury, where they were training to be sent to the front line.

My being in London meant that I got to see him quite often, it being easier for him to get to London when he had leave than travel all the way back to Lancashire. One of the main advantages of that was that he would take me out to lunch. We could also have quite frank discussions about the progress of the war, without worrying about upsetting Mummy.

February 1st, 1941. Went up to town... Waited at the Berkeley for a bit until Daddy arrived – on his way from Salisbury to Carlisle for a fortnight's PAD (Passive Air Defence, army ARP) and we had sherry and gin-and-it, and rang up Meg Berry, who came along and we had a hasty lunch (smoked salmon, Russian salad and coffee) ... Daddy – as indeed the whole nation – prophesies the invasion in the near future: also that Hitler will use gas. Daddy says mustard-gas, and that one needn't be terrified of it, because as long as one wears talc-goggles (which I have) so that it can't blind one, the effects wear off in a day or two. He is very confident that the invasion will be crushed flat, though they may do quite a lot of killing and destroying first (I think most of us feel this) and that, as Hitler always does what is obviously coming a few weeks before it is expected, it will be very soon. (Col Knox or Stimpson (I always muddled them) says 60-90 days: the papers say the first fine day – today was fine, actually: but not early in the morning, which is his usual starting time. Not a single warning all the afternoon! I said I was set on staying put here during the invasion, which he agreed to. Darling Daddy, he is so sensible...

We went out to the station and I saw him off. We were both entirely cheerful – particularly at the last moment when a woman came casually down the crowded platform pushing a hand truck on which was a rather small coffin! Quite incredibly informal and cheering for the about-to-travellers... one seems to have got so used to the idea that there may not be a next time that one doesn't think about it now… Blitzless night so far. The Slough balloon barrage looked rather lovely swimming in clear golden-green light.

What scares me most about this invasion is that I shall do something silly because I shall be frightened and excited. That is much more worrying than the actual invasion, though I don't look forward to that. If it only goes according to our plan: if only we don't muddle it: if only something would happen to prevent it: if only we could set the sea on fire around our coasts or theirs or both, when they were half-way. I wish it was May and all this scare was over.

Monday, February 3rd, 1941. Woken out of very pleasant dream by Miss Bain, who said, "The Wardens asked us to warn you that the Government _particularly_ want everyone to carry their gas-masks _everywhere_. They aren't broadcasting it on the wireless or the Press because they don't want to create a panic."

Snowing again and bitterly cold. Mondays are hell at the best of times… Sudden violent outbursts from naval guns during afternoon, after which the sirens went and there was much aerial activity. We have awfully little blitz now – for the last two weeks. Nothing at night, excited air chief says it is due to the weather, and our aggressive activity has also been restricted…So far no invasion.

Wednesday, February 19th, 1941. Went up to town on Sunday and met Daddy at the Cumberland. He is on his way back from a PAD course at Naworth Castle, near Carlisle, to Salisbury. The course seems to have been quite

fantastic, chiefly on account of the extraordinary ineffi-
ciency and attitude of the 2nd in command: run on the
lines of a prep school for very small boys.

At a meeting of staff and students (all the students
were officers, many wearing last war-ribbons, majors
downward) one student officer asked if they might use the
classrooms as a passage to their bedrooms, instead of going
round outside. The CO said, "I think Major Black has an
objection to that?" B (the 2nd) said, "Yes. I went into the
classrooms a few evenings ago and found officers playing –
actually, playing with the chairs!"

Daddy and Capt Lewis – who joined us – had lots of
other incredible details of life at the castle, during which
they had learnt nothing except how not to run a PAD
school. We had sherries etc in the fourchette bar, and a
lovely lunch – hors d'oeuvre, whitebait and gratin dau-
phinois, by which time we were so full we couldn't face
an ice. It was lovely. Pet of a waiter, and hotel very full
and warm (officers of every nation, Polish navy, Czechs,
Dutch and Belgian, RAF pilots and all kinds of British – all
talking their own languages). I wore new navy coat over
new grey Lafayette frock, very dashing navy hat, with navy
scarf, gloves, belt, bag and navy suede shoes. Effect rather
ravishing, I thought.

Capt Lewis went about 2.30, and Daddy and I walked
round the park… Tea with Aunt Gioia and nice man called
McManus, friend of Uncle Tom's, who does ciphers at the
War Office, so as Aunt Gioia said, anything one said to
him was tactless… Uncle Tom has got new very hush-hush

job. Daddy saw me off at Cavendish Square, and was very cheerful till after the bus had moved off, when I was pulled into depression…

Got back about 7.30, descending from bus with very friendly man who had borrowed my matches in the bus. Far, far too gallant and rather intoxicated: pressed me to have drinks at the French Horn with him, but firmly refused. Suggested another night but I was firm. Tried to persuade me to let him walk home with me, but I was firm, and the call of the French Horn was too strong for him, so we parted – with some relief on my part! Shall have to be careful in this hat!

…On Tuesday Miss Jenkins came down and rang a bell, on which we all put on our gas masks and sat in them for 25 minutes till she rang another bell, when we emerged, realising how far, far better it would be to let the gas do its worst. Mine presses on my eyes so that I can only see when breathing out, and unless held on, slips off my chin. Most miserable creation.

CHAPTER THIRTY-FOUR

Jean

While Pat was enjoying her time in London, I was still at school. We knew the war was no laughing matter, but in typical British style, humour was deployed whenever possible. One Saturday in March 1941, *The Telegraph* ran an article that had its readers chuckling. It was a report on a German initiative to prepare its soldiers for a successful invasion of Britain, which was apparently still pending. *The Telegraph* journalist framed the scheme thus:

"TEACHING NAZIZ 'ENNGGLISCH': INVASION GUIDE"

From our own correspondent. New York. Friday.
Germany has produced a book of phonic phrases for soldiers who, she likes to think, will one day invade Britain. Quotations from it were cabled today by United States correspondents in Berlin...
Kerschn, schlatt aop! Juh ahr mi priseners.
(Caution! Shut up! You are my prisoners!)
Prenauns disstinktlee (pronounce distinctly)
Ai doont noh matsch ov thee Enngglisch lengwidsch (I don't know much of the English language).

Fortunately, the Germans had no need of these useful phrases.

There were signs that perhaps not all was well in the German camp. On May 10th, 1941, Hitler's deputy, Rudolf Hess, made a solo flight across the North Sea towards Britain. As he drew near the coast, his approach was spotted by the RAF who sent Spitfires to intercept him. The interception failed and Hess flew on to Scotland, where he was met by No 141 Squadron RAF. Short of fuel, Hess parachuted from his plane. The plane crashed but Hess landed safely, but for an injury to his foot. He was discovered by a local farmer, who alerted the home guard.

Hess – who was claiming to be a Luftwaffe pilot called Horn – had almost made it to his destination – Dungavel House, home of the Duke of Hamilton. Hess's intention, outlined in a letter addressed to Hitler he had left behind in Germany, was to petition the Duke of Hamilton to help him negotiate peace. When he read the letter, Hitler was predictably furious. Meanwhile, Hess was refused access to the Duke and was imprisoned.

Despite his protestations that he had flown to Scotland in search of reconciliation and an end to the war, at the Nuremberg trials Hess was given a life sentence for crimes against peace. He died – taking his own life – in prison in 1987. To this day, mystery surrounds his ill-fated mission, but I wonder whether he used any of the phonic phrases in the German's invasion phrasebook.

Betrayed by Hess, Hitler had other things to worry about.

In June, the Germans invaded Russia. Prime Minister Churchill made a stirring speech declaring that we would aid Russia while still maintaining our loathing for the Bolshevist Regime under Stalin. It was a very strange change in the international situation, to have Russia as one of the Allies. Was this what Uncle Tid had predicted, we wondered. Would having Russia as an ally eventually lead to the 'triumph of Bolshevism in Europe'?

CHAPTER THIRTY-FIVE

Pat

I had my own, more local concerns. '…clothes-rationing came in at Whitsun: complete bolt from the blue. I still have all my coupons – 26, to last till August. But one gets appallingly little for a coupon – a woman fully dressed is wearing more than a year's allowance worth!'

I had good reason to worry that I could not buy myself a new wardrobe. I was about to start my first job. I wrote: 'I turned 18 last Thursday and am now in a job – started June 15th (my last day as 17). It is with Pearn, Pollinger and Higham, the literary agents. Today I moved from St Hubert's to 15, Park Road, Surbiton. I have a nice room on the ground floor, and everyone is very kind to me because I am so young (ha! Ha!) sometimes it is an advantage to have a baby-face!'

It was a very interesting role in which to begin my working life. Pearn, Pollinger and Higham had a distinguished roster of clients, including Dorothy L. Sayers, various Sitwells and John Gielgud. Once upon a time I had been impressed by John Gielgud, but soon I was writing in my diary, 'Ordinary day. Gielgud rang up once or twice, otherwise little of interest.'

With a little money in my pocket and whole weekends to

spend at leisure, I did my best to enjoy whatever London had to offer and in many ways life was very good indeed. The theatres had reopened, which pleased me enormously. I saw the Beggar's Opera at Sadlers Wells. On Saturdays, my friend Margaret and I would have lunch at a Lyons tea house. There were still Knickerbocker Glories and the tea-house orchestra played, 'lazy as usual, but did play Liebestraum and Schubert serenade between long pauses for recuperation'.

The Germans and Russians continued to square up to one another along an enormous front. The change in play that had seen Russia turn from Germany to become one of the Allied Powers caused headaches for some. I wrote in my diary on June 29th: 'Apparently the poor old BBC was in a fair state about what anthem to play at the end of the usual string of anthems on Sunday evenings, both the International and the old Tsarist hymn being unsuitable, so finally decided on a Cossack march!'

Monday June 30th was the anniversary of the infamous Night of the Long Knives, when Hitler consolidated his power with a purge of the Nazi leadership, including Ernst Rohm, leader of the Sturmabteilung – the paramilitary wing of the Nazi party. Also on the 29th, I wrote:

It's also seven years tomorrow since Hitler's bloodbath on June 30th, 1934. I wonder whether he's thinking of that tonight. I wonder where von Rohm's spirit is – I could hazard a guess! No, I couldn't. I have no idea. We live on the brink of darkness in a little glare of light like

*one searchlight that shines on an empty stage. And then
the light goes out, suddenly, and we don't know anything
more, only darkness. There isn't any heaven or hell, only
darkness. Nothing else that matters, for ever and ever and
ever amen!*

I vacillated between such pessimism and happier moods.
London was bruised and battered after all those months of
airborne attacks but she was still the city I had longed for and
come to love. As well as getting a new job, I had moved to
another boarding house – this time in South London – and my
journey into work meant crossing the river. 'I've seldom seen
anything so lovely as the River this morning when we were
walking across Waterloo Bridge,' I observed. 'The sky was
steel-grey with pale-gold clouds, and the noise and buildings
and bridges were different depths of the same grey, except for
one patch of liquid gold-dust on the water, in front of St Paul's.
And all the little tugs and barges streaming up and down.'

The Russians were fighting with tremendous courage and
the Germans were feeling the pain. By the end of June, I
noted: 'I'm glad to hear however that the Germans have lost
2,000 tanks, 1,500 aircraft, and innumerable killed, wounded
and captured. We continue to make extremely heavy daylight
sweeps over Germany and N France, also night attacks...'

But the truth was that the war was far from over, and that
same night, listening to the radio, I heard The Viscount
Margesson, Churchill's Secretary of State for War, making
an appeal for volunteers, specifically female volunteers, to
join the Auxiliary Territorial Service. It was not the most

rousing call to arms – I called it uninspiring – but it left me thinking, 'For my peace of mind, I ought to join the ATS, WRENS, WAAFS or something.' Not long afterwards, I acted on that thought.

It was traditional for the Owtram men to join the army. At my age, my mother had joined the Women's Land Army. Now she was working as an ARP warden. Aunt Ellie wrote suggesting that I join 'a crowd of jolly girls' who were working for the Foreign Office at a large country house in Buckinghamshire. I replied by telegram, saying 'hate crowds of jolly girls'. Years later, I would discover that that house in Buckinghamshire was in fact Bletchley Park.

In the spring of 1942, I turned to the maternal side of the family for inspiration. As captain of HMS Faulknor, Uncle Tid was naturally very keen that I should join the Women's Royal Navy. He persuaded my mother that the Wrens would look after me and shortly afterwards I was called for an interview in Liverpool. I was worried that the recurrent bouts of bovine TB that had plagued my teenage years might prove an obstacle to my signing up but it turned out that the WRN recruitment board were much more interested in my language skills than my health. They were looking for young women who were competent in German. Thanks to Lilly and Edie, I fit the bill. I was called up in August 1942 and after completing my basic training at HMS Pembroke in Mill Hill, I was sent on a top-secret course set in an unassuming requisitioned house in Wimbledon. Thus began a very exciting period in my life.

CHAPTER THIRTY-SIX

Jean

1942 was a very difficult year for our family. In September 1941, our father's regiment had been sent to the Far East, to defend Singapore. In February 1942, we heard that the Japanese had captured the city state, taking many Allied soldiers prisoner. We had no idea whether Daddy was dead or alive. It would be a very long time before we did.

I was still at school when Singapore fell, as was Bob, though we both longed to be at Newland Hall with our mother and Grandboffin while we waited for news from the Far East. I was desperately unhappy to be so far from home but my teachers and my school friends rallied round. I also had the comfort of my faith.

Since I was a small child sitting in the family pew at St Mark's in Dolphinholme, I had always found comfort in religion. Faced with so much uncertainty, I turned to the church again and saw God's hand in the kindness of the people at The Laurels, who helped me through those early days of not knowing what had happened to Daddy. Pat and I wrote to each other often in the months that followed and, understandably, there were some bleak moments as we wondered whether we would ever see our father again.

Pat had a very different view on religion to me. In April,

two months after the terrible news from Singapore, I wrote to her, wanting to share with her some of the support I had been finding in prayer. In answer to her question 'who is God?', I suggested the following, which was giving me strength during the long wait for news.

I think of God as a combination of all the qualities I most admire as they are shown in the people I love and respect. Then I can worship God because he is my own personal god and my ideal. He doesn't appear the same to everyone because other people haven't the same scale of values. But I believe that he is essentially a kind power, and all the other qualities such as loyalty and courage and generosity and so on are incorporated in it. It's the kindness tho' that's the most important part. Last term I began to rate kindness at its true value. Love is really the same thing, because it means helping other people and doing all you can for them without necessarily liking them, and that, I think, makes 'God is Love' clearer.

The problem of course is really not so much 'is there a God?' but 'why worship God?' I suppose one could go through life accepting God's presents without stopping to think and without wanting to thank him. But if you do that, you only get a bare 25% of what you might have. When you stop and look at a landscape or listen to a Beethoven Symphony (unless you loathe Beethoven) or eat a strawberry or blackberries and cream or chocolate, or when Brucie the dog expresses pleasure at seeing you, or someone is unexpectedly sympathetic or kind (which always liqui-

dates me!) or the wind brings a lovely smell into your room at night or when you remember something or somewhere you've loved, then don't you sometimes think how lovely it is to be able to experience the pleasure all these sort of things give you?

I've known lots of times when I've just wanted to cry with happiness and something inside me wanted to burst with gladness and gratitude. Then I have to find someone or something to thank, and that's where religion comes in. It's no good going up to someone and saying 'thank you for that tree' because (apart from the risk of a mental certificate) they didn't give it to you. You must have a higher power to thank for everything and also to ask for what you want that no-one can give you.

Often it's quite useless asking someone for advice because they don't know what to do any more than you do. Often, when you're tired especially, you feel you'll scream if anyone says anything and you want someone to go and complain to but you can't bear any of the people around you. That, I think, is when one should go and find one's God. Not just on Sunday with everyone else, to show off a new hat and sing nice hymns, but always. And thanksgiving and asking for advice + help + understanding = religion. Some people must get more help out of it than others but no-one is complete without it.

I finished the letter by writing, 'Three pages of sermon! What a sister! However it would be a waste of paper not to send it.'

Pat kept the letter for 80 years, so I suppose she didn't feel entirely brow-beaten. I remember that writing my thoughts down gave me a sense of calm and a feeling that all might still be well. There were still difficult times ahead but in May of that year, the Japanese began to release lists, via the Red Cross, of the men, women and children who had been taken captive in Singapore. Our father's name was among them and we felt a surge of hope.

CHAPTER THIRTY-SEVEN

Pat

Graduating from the mysterious training course in Wimbledon in the autumn of 1942, I signed the Official Secrets Act and became an Acting Petty Officer Special Duties (Linguist) 'Y'. One of 'Freddie's Fairies', in reference to Lieutenant LA 'Freddie' Marshall, whose idea it had been to train women to join the 'Y' Service ('Y' being phonetic for WI or Wireless Intercept), which was recruiting people with German language skills to listen in on German naval traffic in the waters around the United Kingdom.

My first posting was to a listening station based in a requisitioned guest house in Withernsea in the East Riding of Yorkshire. I joined a group of Wrens manning the station 24/7, picking up signals from German Motor Torpedo Boats (MTB's or E-Boats) which were laying sea-mines in the North Sea and the Baltic. We had been trained to use HRO radios to tune into their communication channels. When we picked up a signal, we used our German language skills to note down what was being said. Often, it was just a stream of letters in the German phonetic alphabet, as they communicated using the Enigma Code. When we got one of those messages, it was sent straight to Station X (Bletchley Park, though we did not know it then).

From Withernsea, I was sent to a station in Lyme Regis as a newly-minted Petty Officer. There we listened to Kriegsmarine traffic in the Channel and on the Normandy Coast. It was top secret work and we Wrens were encouraged not to wear our uniforms when we weren't on duty and to say that we were 'factory girls on a holiday' if anyone started asking questions while we were in the local town.

From Lyme Regis, I was sent to be trained in 'direction finding' and posted to Abbot's Cliff, at Capel Le Ferne in Kent. On a clear day, from Abbot's Cliff, you could see the coast of France. It was the biggest and busiest station I worked in, especially as D-Day approached. One morning, walking back to my quarters after a night shift, I happened across Churchill himself, walking on the cliff with his colleagues. The station was, given its proximity to occupied France, quite a dangerous place to be. With an American anti-aircraft station nearby and German bombers constantly flying overhead, not for nothing was the part of the Channel we were watching known as 'Hellfire Corner'. One afternoon, a particularly naïve Wren walked into the radio room with an unexploded shell in her hands. You can imagine how quickly we all jumped under our desks.

Despite Hitler's best efforts, I survived my time at Hellfire Corner. After D-Day, the Y Service was disbanded and I was sent to work at the Admiralty in London, where I translated U-Boat instruction manuals from German into English. It was boring work, so I was very pleased to be transferred to SHAEF, the Supreme Headquarters of the Allied Expeditionary Force. There I worked as a researcher, translating files seized from the Gau Baden-Elsass, the Nazi administrative district encompassing the German state of Baden and occupied Alsace. The documents were mostly reports by 'die Zellenleiter', Nazi party members and low-level domestic spies, who were paid to snoop on their neighbours. It was depressing work, sifting through their reports for evidence of war crimes. I stayed at SHAEF until the end of the war.

Shortly after the war, Freddie Marshall wrote a letter of thanks to his fairies, telling us, 'Like all good fairies you'll live forever.' If only that were true. Of the 400 young women Freddie trained for the 'Y' Service, I know of only a handful who are living still, including myself and my friend Pam Harding, who has recently turned 102.

CHAPTER THIRTY-EIGHT

Jean

I left school in the summer of '42 but was still too young to join the women's forces. Stuck at home, I tried to make myself useful, helping Grandboffin with his animals, but not knowing the fate of our father since the Fall of Singapore made joining the war effort seem much more urgent. When I received an invitation to interview to join the FANY – the First Aid Nursing Yeomanry – on my 18th birthday, I was overjoyed. I immediately made arrangements to go to London.

I didn't know much about the FANY when I applied to join. I learned that it had been established in 1907, as a cavalry of nurses who helped bring wounded soldiers from the field. Early recruits were expected to have their own horse.

My interview went well, though there were a couple of questions that struck me as odd at the time. One was whether I liked to do crosswords. I thought my interviewers must have run out of things to ask me.

It all became clear after I completed my basic training at Overthorpe Hall near Banbury and was sent to train as a code and cipher officer. My first position was at the SOE's headquarters on Baker Street. The SOE – the Special Operations Executive, or Ministry of Ungentlemanly Warfare, as it was sometimes known, ran agents embedded with resistance groups behind enemy lines. Before I could work there, I had to sign the Official Secrets Act. I had never felt quite so important.

At Baker Street I worked at decoding and coding messages between Britain and the underground resistance movements in Holland and Belgium. It was an interesting job, but when I saw that the FANY were looking for volunteers to go overseas, I jumped at the chance.

Our mother wasn't entirely happy at the thought of my going abroad – by now we knew that my father was in a prisoner of war camp – but Grandboffin persuaded her that I should be allowed to go and not long afterwards, I boarded the MV Stirling Castle, a liner turned troop ship in Liverpool for a destination still unknown. The only clue was that we had been given a summer uniform to wear when we got there. We FANYs had been made officers so that we could have cabins on the officers' deck of the ship to keep us out of trouble!

It turned out that we were on our way to Egypt. I couldn't believe my luck, ending up somewhere so very different from Lancashire. It was also somewhere I had always wanted to visit, having heard so much about Egypt from the traders that supplied raw cotton to Cliff Mill. In Cairo, I was tasked with coding messages to brief Albanian and Italian allies. In my spare time, I met my friends at the glamorous Gezira Club and saw the pyramids by moonlight. Then, when Southern Italy was liberated, the centre for coordinating the Balkan Resistance was moved there and I followed. I was based in

Torre a Mare, where I coded correspondence with the Yugo-slavian partisans, just over the Adriatic. It was in Italy that I found myself working for Fitzroy Maclean, whom Churchill had entrusted with Britain's relationship with Josep Tito, the Yugoslav partisan leader.

My work in Italy was tremendously important. I was sending coded messages to coordinate drops of food, medical supplies and ammunition. The stakes were very high. The agents with whom we corresponded were risking their lives and we dreaded hearing the terrible news that one had been lost. The stress was enormous which was perhaps reflected in the way we partied whenever we weren't on a shift, drinking and smoking in the officers' mess. There was bad behaviour. Still only 19, I sometimes found it hard to repel the advances of amorous Allied servicemen.

I made the most of my time in Italy. The people were very friendly and I loved the weather and the landscape. Whenever I had leave, I would catch a lift to Naples to see an opera. I also hitchhiked to Florence where I had the Duomo almost to myself – there was just one other worshipper inside the great cathedral. Strictly speaking, I wasn't supposed to be in Florence, which was much too close to the front-line to be safe, but my youth and inexperience made me brave, even when I saw my first dead body by the side of the road.

When Germany surrendered and the war ended in Europe in May 1945, I watched the celebratory fireworks over Bari. It was a bittersweet moment, knowing that the fighting continued in South East Asia, where our father was still held captive in a Japanese prison camp. It wasn't until

August that the Japanese surrendered and Daddy and his men were finally free.

Not long after that the office in Italy was closed down and I boarded a troop ship from Naples back home. I was sad to say goodbye to Italy but very excited to see my father again. Pat and I were both in Lancashire to welcome him home in October 1945, both of us wearing our uniforms. It was a wonderful day.

Having Daddy back was a dream come true. However life in Lancashire soon seemed very flat after the excitement of Cairo and Italy. What on earth was I going to do next?

PART THREE
After the War

CHAPTER THIRTY-NINE

Pat

I was demobbed in the summer of 1945 but didn't have long to wait until my next adventure, working as a junior archivist at the newly reopened British Embassy in Oslo, where my godmother Aunt Ellie's husband was ambassador. It was an interesting time to be in Norway. The Norwegians led the world in the production of 'heavy water', deuterium oxide, to be used in nuclear power and atomic weapons. During the War, the Allies had bombed Norway's heavy water production facilities to prevent the Germans, who occupied the country, from harnessing the technology for their own war effort. Now the industry was the focus of new peacetime activity.

I met many fascinating people at the embassy, including the Norwegian resistance hero Max Manus and the British conductor Malcolm Sargent, who visited Oslo on a concert tour. Though my official title was 'junior archivist', I was really more of a social secretary to Aunt Ellie. Mostly I filed things, made tea and helped with the sealing of diplomatic bags – an occult mystery involving candle, pincers and special kinds of knots, only known to the senior archivists. I had a little apartment in a street that was called Cort Adeleragate at one end and Kort Adeleragate at the other, owing to the Norwegian spelling reform.

While I was there, Jean came out to visit and we spent my leave in Denmark. It was wonderful to be able to spend time with my sister away from the shadow of war. We decided to get there by train, stopping in Gothenburg on the way, carrying a dress-box full of banana sandwiches – 48 of them to be precise – left over from a party at the Embassy.

Travelling through Sweden and Denmark so soon after the war involved a much greater degree of organisation than it would today. In particular, there were rules about how much currency one could take. I'd made a trip to the bank a couple of days before we left, to pay the rent on my flat, pick up some travellers' cheques and get a certificate regarding the Norwegian kroner we intended to take with us. I was also worried about my new fur jacket (I should note that at that time, fur was commonly worn in Scandinavia. Now I have very firm convictions about animal welfare and would not wear it).

Someone had told us that Copenhagen was much smarter than Oslo, and at the last minute, I had decided to take my newly-acquired double silver-fox fur, in spite of the fact that it was midsummer and extremely hot. I discovered very late that you had to have furs documented before taking them across any frontier, so at the last minute, Jean and I galloped up and down the platform, beseeching anyone who happened to be wearing any kind of uniform to do something about mine, which I brandished eagerly at them to make our desires clear.

I remember approaching the guard, several mailmen and the engine driver, while Jean – newer to the country – pursued high officers of the Norwegian army and air force. None of these, though sympathetic, seemed to have any idea how to deal with the situation. I began to have awful visions of my jacket being seized and impounded at the first frontier.

Then, to our great relief, there appeared on the scene my friend from the Belgian embassy, a tall and striking figure in riding breeches. He was extremely soothing. We might be more tranquil as *this*, he said, referring to my jacket, was obviously second-hand fur (I had hoped no one would realise), of an inferior kind and quite unsaleable, and no one would worry. It was only expensive furs they worried about. I thanked him, rather crestfallen.

We boarded a night train from Oslo. Nothing happened till we reached the Swedish frontier, where officials came along to check our money and passports. Before they had time to ask for them, I handed over our travellers' cheques and the statement about our Norwegian kroner. This last they gazed thoughtfully at for a long time and handed back without comment. No trouble at all travelling, Jean and I pointed out to each other after they left, as long as you have everything properly planned and documented in advance. We slept through Sweden and entered Denmark at Helsingor. More officials roused us and the currency inspector gazed even longer at my statement from the Realbank, scratched his head, called another official who also came and gazed at it, and both consulted together in Danish.

'Do you think there's anything wrong?' enquired Jean from the berth below.

'There couldn't be,' I said confidently. 'They're probably just not used to people remembering these things.'

Finally they shook their heads and handed the slip of paper back. I had a look at it myself. It had the Realbank's heading all right, but it was a receipt for last month's rent to my apartment at Kort Adeleragate 12.

Arriving in Copenhagen, we had a huge breakfast at the hotel opposite the station (I regret to say we left the last 20 banana sandwiches on the train) and were interested to see that the ladies at the next table followed up their breakfasts with full-size cigars. We debated about this but decided not.

We got the address of some rooms from the bureau near the station which existed to supply them (a very efficient bit of tourist service) and moved in. The rooms overlooked a square lake in the middle of the city. The landlady, who was young and charming, was renting out rooms on the quiet while her husband was away on a business trip, to make herself some money. She implored us, for this reason, not to let anyone else know the address and telephone number, as her husband would be furious if he found out. We saw her point, though it was a slightly inconvenient arrangement. But the room was delightful, and she gave us enormous breakfasts, coffee and a heap of different kinds of hot rolls with butter and jam and whipped cream.

When so much of Europe was still in post-war gloom, Copenhagen seemed a wonderful, colourful city. In the intervals of sightseeing, we ate strawberries and cream at sidewalk café tables, and when a British cruiser came in, bearing some naval cadets we knew, we went to dances on board. The cadets showed us how you raised and lowered the guns and swung them from side to side. 'And how do you actually fire them?' asked Jean.

Our cadets fiddled with this and that level, caught each other's eyes and finally explained, embarrassingly, 'Well, we haven't actually got to that part yet.'

We were rather touched to see how many little Danish boys had been stuffed into miniature British sailors' uniforms by their mothers in honour of the cruiser's visit – rather surprised too, when the Little Rock came in on a fleet visit a couple of days later, how quickly the little Danes appeared dressed in American naval uniform.

One very hot day, we decided to swim in the warm and shallow Baltic. We found there was one bathing place for men and one for women, boarded off at a little distance from each other, as people in Scandinavia prefer to bathe nude. Matrons lay packed like stranded whales along the board-walks, and it was all very discreet and segregated, except for the seaward end of the enclosure, which was open, and opposite which a row of little boats sat bobbing and no doubt observing the spectacle through binoculars.

We went out to visit the castle at Hillerod on its lake, and managed to leave my camera in the train going and my sister's in the train coming back. We had some difficulty in telephoning the people we had introductions to, owing to the peculiar Danish system of counting, by which 50, for instance, is half 60 on the telephone and after a number of unsatisfactory conversations with strangers we fell back on dialling the operator and beginning cautiously with, 'Kann De snakker Engelsk?'

Our cadets invited us out to a final dinner. We had rationed our kroner to so many a day, but for this occasion I bought a ravishing little white straw hat trimmed with white feathers, which was not altogether popular with Jean, as we both had to live on her allocation for the next two days. However, she was very nice about it and the cadets liked the hat.

Eventually the cadets sailed for England and we had to depart to Norway. The Danish shops were, as the Norwegian ones weren't at that time, full of food, especially dairy produce. We had brought a spare rucksack in anticipation of this, and we packed it full of cheeses, bacon, and several dozen eggs. We took all our baggage down to the station and left it in the care of two porters, with instructions to meet us at the train.

We arrived at our compartment, but there were no porters. The clock-hand crept towards the minute of departure but there were still no porters. People began to say goodbye and the guard, watch in hand, stood poised to wave his flag – still no porters. We besought the guard not to let the train leave. But this was an international train, he said; it was impossible to hold it. Other officials and interested passengers became involved in the situation. The minute of departure was well past when finally our porters ambled into view far down the platform. They were urged to hurry and sharply upbraided by various officials, but as far as we could tell, they gave as good as they got, and heaving our baggage aloft, flung it violently into the baggage car. There was an ominous scrunch as the rucksack hit the back wall – our eggs, our eggs!

We spent the ferry crossing from Helsingor to Helsingborg picking dozen after dozen of sticky broken eggs out of the rucksack and dropping them into the Skagerrak while the other passengers looked on in astonishment. Not one egg survived.

We arrived in Gothenburg early in the morning and were taking the evening train to Oslo. Gothenburg was a very clean, plain city with handsome buildings, streets that looked as if they were swept every morning, and appropriate citizens. As soon as the British consulate opened, we were there to collect our kroner, and spent a happy morning shopping. We also bought a new camera and some film and had lunch at a pastry shop called Brautigan's: after which, counting our kroner, we found we had just enough for a sandwich each before catching our train at nine in the evening, but not an ore more.

We couldn't afford a visit to the cinema, we were too tired of walking to feel like a museum, we didn't know anybody, but we had to do something to fill our remaining eight hours on Swedish soil without having to pay to do it. It was exceedingly hot, and for some reason we had dressed ourselves up in silk dresses, gloves, stockings, high heels and large straw hats. We looked smart all right but we were also hot, cross and tired. We decided we had better stay away from shops, so – as being the one thing which was free – we wandered into a park in the middle of the town and eventually came to rest on a little wooden jetty beside a quiet path at the edge of a canal. As it was so hot, we took off our gloves, hats, shoes and stockings and put them on the bank, dangling our feet in the water and talked. It was really very pleasant.

At regular half-hour intervals a booming sound was heard, and then a small motorboat full of tourists came round the corner of the canal, passed us, and disappeared round the next bend. A man with a megaphone in the bow was describing points of interest to the tourists, but the man who worked the motor was very bored, and waved to us, shrugged his shoulders and spread his hands. So we waved back each time. It seemed to cheer him up. He also made vivid diving gestures at us, suggesting that it would be nice for us to plunge out of the hot sun into the cool canal, and we would nod vigorously in agreement.

This went on till about seven, when we decided we might as well buy our sandwiches and eat them slowly. So we picked up our shoes and stockings and retired decorously into the bushes to put them on, leaving our hats on the bank. While we were thus ambushed, the motorboat came round again. We noticed that our little man was looking out for us, but of course all that could be seen was our two hats, sitting on the bank. A look of consternation came over his face, which gradually developed into horror, and he rose to his feet and stood grasping his motor and scanning the water up and down, obviously under the impression that we had taken his advice and dived in, and, poor wretches, failed to come up. We murmured to each other that we really ought to let him know, but by then he was swept relentlessly away on his course, still gazing wildly around. So we picked up our hats and headed for the railway station.

We crossed the frontier all right on the receipt for my rent, but the inspector picked up my fur and looked doubtfully at it. 'Didn't anyone tell you this ought to be documented?' he asked.

'It's just a second-hand one,' I explained.

'That makes no difference,' he said sternly. 'This is probably dutiable. It is obviously an expensive fur.'

CHAPTER FORTY

Pat

Joining the WRNS had changed my life forever, not least because it made me eligible for the ex-Service grant that paid for me to study English Literature at St Andrews. The ex-service grant scheme was very enlightened and allowed a great many people of my generation to access an education they might not otherwise have had. I no longer needed to worry that the family only had enough money to pay for my little brother's university years. For my three courses a year, I paid £21.

Scottish universities, unlike Oxford and Cambridge, followed the continental system of giving a broad rather than a specialised education. On the arts side, it was obligatory to take five different courses in your first two years, including compulsory Latin and philosophy. After that you 'majored' in one of the courses elected. There was no tutorial system and instruction was entirely given in lectures.

I lodged in a garret, the attic in a fisherman's cottage on North Street, one of the three oldest streets of St Andrews, and although it did not exactly command a view of the sea, by climbing onto the sink and craning out of the window towards the left, you could see the silver sheen of the bay through the trees growing among the ruins of the cathedral.

Twisting yourself the other way, you could see the grey tower of the university church. That grey tower had a clock on it, and my day usually started with an acrobatic inspection of this; if I woke at nine, a sharp sprint along North Street would get me to the college quadrangle in time for a lecture starting at five past.

I rented my room, together with a loft for keeping coal in and a very small WC, for one pound a week from Mrs Fisher, who lived in two second-floor rooms below it and had the wonderfully lilting voice of East Fife that must have got some of its tones from the gulls that swoop down the windy streets and carry on screaming arguments among the town's garbage pails.

'Bye-bye the noo!' Mrs Fisher would shrill up the stone stair. 'I'm just goin' down the toon!'

If I had visitors talking too late, she would bang on the ceiling of her room with a broomstick which she must have kept beside the bed for the purpose. But she was kindness itself, in the practical unsentimental way of east-of-Scotland people. So were all the people in our block. They had true neighbourliness without pretension.

You would see this whenever there were chimney fires. All the houses were old, and they all had open fires, and the chimneys were always catching fire. The fire brigade was prompt in getting there as soon as a fire was reported, but they charged you five shillings for putting it out, so the neighbours would hurry to help you get it under control before the brigade heard about it. You would be in Mrs Broon's grocery shop waiting your turn when a child would come flying in.

'Mrs Henderson! Your chimney's on fire!'

'Och, jings. Has it been reportit?'

Our particular block consisted of cottages surrounding a stone-paved courtyard which was used for drying nets in when St Andrews was a fishing town. At least six families lived there. Between them they had produced a surprising number of tough, noisy little boys in hobnailed boots, all about the same age, who ran in and out incessantly, accompanied by an assortment of bedraggled, cheerful dogs, scattering the cats of the establishment before them in startled leaps to the roof of the washhouse.

On the windowsills of the front houses there would usually be sitting one or two ancient mariners in thick blue jerseys, gazing thoughtfully across at the Old Castle Tavern opposite. They could remember the days before the herring moved away, when the fishing fleet used to go out in all its grandeur from the harbour, now silted up, and all along the sidewalks the fishwives would be sitting at their tubs in their big aprons and caps and striped skirts, cleaning and packing the fish and sending backchat flying to and fro in their high, harsh voices.

St Andrews has always been a religious centre from the time of St Regulus or Rule, bringing the relics of St Andrew to Scotland. He built a chapel over them on the seaward tip of the cliff. In the middle ages an enormous cathedral grew slowly up on the rock, surrounded by the refectories, cells and offices of the community which served it, the whole area being surrounded by a high curtain wall, pierced with slots for archers and with towers towards the sea, which still stand. To the landward side, a city grew, with three streets which converge at the west door of the cathedral.

The tower of the cathedral was not well built, and toppled down in some north sea gale. A similar fate befell the old castle. The castle, with its sheltering walls and sunny corners, made a delightful retreat for reading during the summer term – particularly if you found a spot out of earshot of the official guide, who took bunches of visitors round at half-hourly intervals: 'Here, ladies and gentlemen, you see the original Bottle Dungeon, the only one of its kind in the country, which is of course a replica of the one at Rome… and the Archbishop's body was hung out of the very same window by one arm and one leg in the shape of a St Andrew's cross…' I learned that tour guide's spiel by heart.

On a winter's morning, I would get up to the sound of the wind whistling up the stone stairs from the yard, rattling under my door, and out again through the window and the open chimney in a perfect circular draught. Hurrying to a lecture, one would be glad of the scarlet, full-length woollen gown with its purple velvet collar and yoke which all St Andrews' undergraduates wore – originally so that they could be sighted at a distance by their instructors, malingering on the golf-course or sneaking into a town tavern – I doubt whether they were very practical, with their loose flapping sleeve-flaps, for playing golf.

With Beowulf and Wright's *Anglo Saxon Grammar* tucked under my arm, I would join the scarlet-clad throng pouring into the college quadrangle, circling the green lawn and taking short cuts through the grey cloisters, and into a lecture room which was often so crowded that the only space left was perched on a high windowsill. As ten o'clock approached, one's thoughts would turn towards coffee, and five minutes before the hour the whole room would start a steady stamping to remind the lecturer his time was nearly up. In Scottish universities, approval and enthusiasm were expressed by stamping, and it was also used to draw the authorities' attention to anything – like the fact that it was five to ten. Released, we would stream away to whichever of the 27 coffee shops of the town we frequented. One was patronised mostly by the athletes, the square-shouldered highland footballers, and their entourages; another one by the dramatic society. A third café was shared, oddly enough, by the Catholics and the Communists. This was the one which I (though neither a Catholic nor a Communist) usually went to.

On Sundays, back in my garret, I would build a fire of driftwood collected from the beach, the salt on it burning with a blue and green flame. There was a heavy, round table with an ink-stained green cloth on which we edited the university magazine, College Echoes. College Echoes came out seven times a year, and every other editorial was devoted to heartrending appeals to new talent to show itself ('this is your magazine. Perhaps the last issue didn't interest you – why not help to write the next?') but it always boiled down to the faithful brigade of old hacks producing most of the contents. One of these myself, I sometimes sat down in front of the fire faced with the desperate necessity of writing a poem three inches long in eight-point type to fill the gap left by the failure of the Scottish Nationalist Society to turn in their report.

The old grey town, the scarlet gowns, the blue sea, the long white sands, the wind blowing down the street with the tang of seaweed covered rocks in it or with the chill of the late snow on the Sidlaw Hills to the north across two rivers... I loved it all. My years at St Andrews were a very happy time indeed.

In the summer of 1951, I left St Andrews with a 1st Class Honours degree and moved to Oxford, where I was to study for a B. Litt in English at Somerville College, which was at that time one of very few Oxford colleges to admit female students.

It was lovely to be in Oxford, not least because our little brother Bob had recently arrived in the city as an under-graduate at Christ Church college and we were soon joined by Jean, who had found herself a job working as assistant to the university's vice-chancellor. Bob was a member of the Oxford University Boat Club and Jean and I often went down to the river to watch him row in college races. Being so close to both my siblings again was wonderful. I especial-ly enjoyed the opportunity to have supper anywhere but in Somerville's dining room, where fish pie with a topping of cornflakes was one of the chef's specialties.

I spent two years at Oxford and by the time I finished my B. Litt, I had spent six years in education. I jumped at the chance to stay in academia, crossing the Atlantic to take a Masters in American Literature at Harvard.

CHAPTER FORTY-ONE

Jean

As a child, I had thought that I would like to become a farm-er but the war – specifically my time with the FANY – had changed the course of my life too. Now I knew that more than anything, what I really wanted was to travel. Spending time in Cairo and Italy had taken me away from my safe Lancashire upbringing and shown me that there was much to be explored. I also wanted to continue to be of some sort of service to people in need.

After I was demobbed from the FANY, I was offered oppor-tunities to stay overseas but our mother was insistent. Daddy was coming home from three years in a prisoner of war camp and he would want to spend time with his family – including me and Pat. To ensure that I would be around, to begin with I worked in London – first at a company called Ibbs and Tillett, which organised the careers of various musicians, later with a charity that helped refugees arriving in Britain to find homes and work. It was interesting work and useful but when, in January 1947, Fitzroy Maclean asked if I would like to join him and his team in Europe, working for the Refugee Com-mission, I jumped at the chance. I received the job offer on a Friday and a couple of days later, I was on a train to Italy.

We started out in Rome, but soon I was working for the

Special Refugee Commission in Austria, where female staff were lodged in a Schloss with mountain views. It seemed like a dream. I wrote to Pat, 'We have meals at a big round table with loads of flowers on it and the most unbelievable view right away over the valley to the mountains of Jugoslavia, and when it's clear in the mornings all the valley is the most wonderful colours with the leaves turned, and in the mountain valleys the clouds come down exactly like pools of milk and just the higher peaks stick out, all grey and seamed and absolutely still, like a painting instead of being a real landscape.'

I was working at that time in the 'Intelligence Section', and tantalisingly added in my letter to Pat, 'I do wish I could tell you about it but once again I'm surrounded by security and the Official Secrets Act and so forth.'

I travelled whenever I could. I made several trips with Pat in the immediate post-war years.

While Pat was in Oslo, I had travelled to meet her there. Later, when Pat was at St Andrews, we spent time in Scotland together. We made a visit to Pitmilly House, a notoriously haunted house just outside the city. I remember one of Pat's friends had a dog with him and as we crossed the threshold, the dog froze with his hackles up and stared at something none of us humans could see. I had been in the presence of evil when I attended a war crimes trial while working in Austria. This felt like something similar to me.

While Pat was studying at Oxford, she was given the opportunity to spend a term at the Sorbonne (where Simone De Beauvoir was lecturing). We caught up with each other in Paris, where we stayed in a curious pension on the Left Bank near the Luxembourg Gardens which had a piano in the bathroom. We weren't allowed to take hot baths, in case the steam rendered the piano out of tune.

It was a very strict pension. The landlady insisted that we join her for dinner each night but we rather resented the eight course meals that inevitably meant we were late for any concert or theatre date.

In Paris, Pat had lectures all week but on Sundays we were free to do as we pleased and we hitchhiked to all sorts of places within a day trip's reach of the city. One weekend, we weren to Chartres with its wonderful cathedral. We got a lift back with some van drivers who were slightly boozy and getting a bit amorous so we got out rather quickly. All the same, I liked Paris so much that I found myself a job there, working for UNESCO, so that I could stay on for a while.

After a short period in Paris, I returned to Britain to take up a career as an almoner in Scotland. The role of an almoner is best described as a 'medical social worker'. I was entrusted with assessing the financial needs and distributing charitable funds to people needing medical care in the days before the NHS made such care free at source. I was horrified at the poverty I came across. People travelled to see me from the furthest outreaches of Scotland. When I visited them in their homes, I saw a world I would not have believed existed in the 20th century. All I really knew of Scotland was the beautiful landscape we had seen on family holidays before the war. Now I saw the rural poverty behind the beauty. It was such a contrast to my comfortable life. I remember visiting some women on a small island and being rather shocked by what they had to cope with but they were very friendly and I think they were as interested in me as I was in them.

Despite coming from such a different background, I seemed to get on with my clients. I had a sense for when I wasn't wanted, at which point I would take myself off to do something else. At the same time, when my help was wanted, I did my very best, supporting them as they looked for work or training courses.

I was able to help one family in particular, when their daughter had a baby. A little while later, the baby's grandfather presented me with a mirror in recognition of my efforts on the family's behalf. On no account was I supposed to accept presents but I knew how much it meant to the man to be able to give me that mirror and so I decided not to turn it down. I still have it.

I knew I'd had a lucky life. I had never been desperately poor. I'd always had a strong family around me. I think that might have helped me to be useful in my work. Because I had a safe background, I didn't have to worry about myself but could put my focus elsewhere. Working with my clients in Scotland was much more interesting than working around smug types who could have whatever they wanted.

I had been brought up with the sense that one should get on with things and help wherever one could. Both our parents were very good organisers, who instilled in us a feeling of responsibility in the wider world. I like people (almost as much as I like dogs). And I like looking after things. Social work suited me very well.

CHAPTER FORTY-TWO

Pat

In 1953, I travelled to the United States to take up my place at Radcliffe College, the women's college affiliated to Harvard. I went by sea, on the Queen Mary, crossing the Atlantic during a hurricane. The weather was at its worst towards the end of the journey. While the first class passengers huddled in their cabins, I went up onto the deck, together with some other students, to watch the huge waves (and get drenched), then took advantage of the fact that all the upper class lounges were empty to experience a bit of luxury. I remember watching a grand piano sliding backwards and forwards across the floor of the ship's ballroom.

Arriving in Boston, I found my lodgings in Brattle Street and settled in. For my first term, I lived in an all women's residence. One night, a man broke into the building through a window but, confronted by the formidable ladies of Radcliffe College, he climbed straight out again.

It was an interesting time to be in the States; particularly at Harvard. McCarthyism was at its height and several of the university's left-leaning professors were under investigation.

I wanted to know as much as I could about American politics. I queued for hours in the cold New England night to hear Adlai Stevenson, who had been the Democrat candidate in the 1952 election and would stand again in 1956, speak at the Sanders Theater on the campus (called the 'yard' at Harvard). The first time we queued, 3,000 students turned up for 1,400 places. After not getting into the lecture and not wanting to hear it over loudspeakers in an adjacent building, we rushed home to listen to the speech on the radio. The following night, my friends and I were able to get into the theatre to hear the great man speak in person. It felt exciting to have been so close to the man who might be the next president of the United States.

I did some public speaking myself at Harvard's English Speaking Union, where I was introduced as 'Pat Oo-trum, who has the most beautiful Scottish accent.' I might have hammed it up a little for my speech on St Andrew's and Oxford.

After leaving Harvard Graduate School with an MA degree in the summer of 1954, I decided to take a road trip. First I visited friends in California. At a cocktail party in Santa Barbara I met Christopher Isherwood, author of 'Goodbye To Berlin', the semi-autobiographical novel which inspired the musical 'Cabaret'. On the way back to the east coast, I stopped in Michigan with the political theorist and literary critic Russell Kirk, author of 'The Conservative', who had been a friend of mine at St Andrews. In Michigan I was thrilled to see a barn-raising. Then I had a few days in New York before sailing home.

Although, with my experience I could have had an academic career, I still wanted to be a journalist and had an interview – in Manhattan's Algonquin Hotel, made famous by Dorothy Parker and her 'Magic Circle' – with the editor of *Newsweek* magazine, who offered me a staff contract. It was tempting, but thinking it over, I could see that if I became an American journalist I should hardly ever see my family in England again and, all things considered, I would rather be an English journalist. The editor entirely understood and wished me 'the best of all possible whirls'. Shortly afterwards, I sailed home on the Queen Elizabeth.

The whole family were on the dock at Southampton to meet me. They fell about laughing in reply to my shouts of 'Hi folks! Great to see you!'

I had come home speaking American.

Back in Lancashire, I started a new job hunt, applying to several papers and magazines. An offer came from *Time and Tide* magazine of a staff writing job at £9 a week. I pointed out that it would be difficult to live in London on £9 a week and they said, 'But you would meet such interesting people!' I wasn't sure that interesting people would be keen to meet someone who couldn't afford to pay for their share of lunch and turned the offer down. At this point I wrote to the *Daily Mail*, explaining that I was inexperienced as a journalist but keen to learn. The editor wrote back saying that the *Mail* wanted a woman reporter for their Manchester office where the reporters were all men. Five days a week and a modest but adequate salary. I accepted.

On the Monday morning I set off over the Bolton Moors to Manchester, 50 miles from our home. I found a bed-sit, but it was next to a plumber's yard and the noise from early morning was so loud I was soon forced to find another; a large first floor room in a house at the end of a leafy cul-de-sac in the suburb of Fallowfield. The only snag was that the tenant of the room opposite had just learned to play the piano but only knew one tune, 'The Dream of Olwen', which he played endlessly. Also the landlord trained racing greyhounds and asked if I could bring some live rabbits from the country for him to practise chasing. Certainly not.

The Daily Mail reporters had desks in one corner of a large open space on the first floor of a building in Deansgate in Central Manchester. *The Daily Sketch* reporters occupied another corner, and on the far side of the room were the messenger boys. If you wanted copy taken to the sub-editors or a mug of tea, you shouted 'boy!' and one of them came over. They very kindly made me a special mug by winding a string round and round the handle.

I learned later that the news that a female was joining them had filled the happy all-male band of reporters with dismay. They had removed the raunchier pin-ups from the notice boards, and one who was cultivating a beard had second thoughts.

I was told that I would be trained by the senior reporter, Harold Pendlebury, and gain law-court experience with the court reporter, Michael Kelly. The first story I was given to write was from an announcement of a survey of women's boots. Harold Pendlebury carefully changed each of my references to 'women's boots' to 'ladies' bootees', much to my annoyance. But I did learn from Harold that you put all the arresting features of a story in the first paragraph, and after that you expanded it. Also that in divorce case reports you could only report what the judge had included in his final summing up.

My favourite stories in those early days were snow stories, when you could go up in a small plane and fly about over the Pennines with a photographer and a road map, working out which villages were cut off and which roads blocked.

Less romantically, in the police courts, sitting alongside Michael Kelly, I discovered that incest was not, as I had thought, only a theme in Renaissance plays – but of course these cases were not reported in *The Daily Mail*. Not in those days.

There was a strict rule about not intruding on private grief, but I soon learned that if a sympathetic female reporter appears on the scene of some catastrophe it is quite common for a victim to want to pour out his or her grief. You just have to write carefully.

The longest-running story during my time with *The Daily Mail* was that of the Vanishing Vicar of Woodford. Woodford is a suburb on the south side of Manchester and its vicar suddenly disappeared without trace. It wasn't long before the whole northern press pack was in pursuit.

The vicar had a daughter about my age and my editor thought she might know something and give us a tip-off. Unfortunately she had a fast sports car and though I spent many an hour beetling after her as fast as my Morris Minor would go, and she was quite friendly whenever I caught up with her, if she knew anything, she wasn't saying. It was a relief when the *Daily Mirror*, given better information, opened the boot of a car, disclosing the missing vicar. I think there was some romance involved.

Our office covered Ireland also and I remember writing up some heiress's party and, as we drove back to Dublin, being puzzled by the small headstones installed at intervals along the roadside. My Irish driver explained that it had once been the route of a tramway and as the local pub-goers made their unsteady way home, they sometimes lay down for a rest and were unfortunately decapitated by the next tram. Most countries would perhaps have put up a fence, but this was Ireland and they put up gravestones. I was reminded of the story of my grandmother Effie and the local man who could never make it home from the pub without going to sleep in a ditch. He was lucky we didn't have trams in Dolphinholme.

Not long after I joined *The Daily Mail* there was a strike in the newspaper industry and we 'wrote for the spike' knowing that our reports wouldn't be published. It gave me a good opportunity to practise writing stories in the paper's style that would not be used.

The news editor had explained on my arrival: 'We don't do fashion, Miss Owtram' (before giving me that story about boots to write). I said, 'thank goodness for that.' However, I could not altogether avoid fashion. Occasionally, when the woman's page editor in Fleet Street was on holiday, I went down to help out in London. There the job was quite unlike general news reporting in Manchester. The atmosphere was very different. In Manchester, a clean mug for my tea was a luxury. In London, you'd arrive in the office to find a single perfect orchid in a box from a designer who wanted his dress show covered. All the same, I was glad to get back to Manchester.

With the university, theatre, newspapers, radio and television, Manchester was a good place to be young. I was on the Press Ball committee, so I have happy memories of it socially as well as professionally. Not least because it was through my time there that I met my husband, Ray Davies.

Ray was the *Daily Mail*'s northern music and entertainment correspondent and as such, he always had spare press tickets for orchestra concerts and new plays, which he generously shared with the rest of us. We became good friends and when rumours began to circulate that Granada TV was planning to open in Manchester – there was no BBC or other television service in the area, and I had only seen rather grainy pictures in the United States – Ray introduced me to Barrie Heads, who was going to be Granada's Head of News and Research.

When Barrie said he was looking for someone to write a documentary script, Ray chipped in with, 'Pat can write' (which was generous of him, as he really could write. Away from the *Daily Mail*, Ray wrote radio scripts for Morecambe and Wise).

Barrie agreed to give me a chance and commissioned some work from me. The first programme he commissioned, to give the outside broadcast unit some experience, was to be 'An Hour in Manchester's Municipal Greenhouse'.

A municipal greenhouse was not a subject offering many dramatic possibilities but I gave it my best try. The producer came from the theatre but had done a short Granada training course (for some reason called 'Viking'), and we worked out the visual angles and made the programme. This led on to other Outside Broadcast stories, including one about the Manchester fire brigade for which we got permission to burn a condemned house. As the programme had to last an hour and the fire brigade was all too efficient, we only just managed to eke out a show by having enough people throwing inflammable material into the flames to last out the time. Another practice programme entitled 'Beauty Becomes You' featured three women of different ages being given facial treatments in Kendal Milne's Beauty Department but in rather grainy monochrome television there was very little perceivable difference from their first appearances to their final ones.

When Granada started transmitting they offered me a contract to produce, first of all, educational programmes, and later on, series for children, then programmes for adult audiences like 'Criss Cross Quiz', 'University Challenge' and advertising 'magazines' which were linked commercials. Seeing such a new and exciting horizon opening up ahead of me, I left the *Daily Mail* for television.

It was interesting work and I covered a huge variety of subjects but I did not expect my knowledge of German to be called into use in such a dramatic way as it did on February 6th 1958. On that dreadful day, a plane carrying the Manchester United football team – The Busby Babes – and various supporters and journalists, crashed during take-off in Munich. The whole of Manchester held its breath as we waited to hear news of the casualties. Using my German, I was able to speak directly to the staff at the German hospital and keep Granada's news room and the team's fans updated. It was a terrible time. Bobby Charlton, who would go on to play in England's triumphant 1966 World Cup team was among the survivors, but of the 44 people on board the plane, 23 died, including eight players and the team's chief coach. Manchester United lost a generation of champions that night and the whole city mourned with them.

At Granada, I had an office adjacent to that occupied by a young scriptwriter called Tony Warren. Though Tony was a decade younger than me, we soon became great friends and would often go out together during the week. Tony was a very interesting man, of great personal integrity. He was openly gay at a time when homosexual acts between men were still illegal.

I remember clearly the day Tony asked me to look over a programme proposal that he had called Florizel Street. It was for a soap opera following the lives of the people living on a single street in the fictional town of Weatherfield, which Tony had based on Salford. Tony had written the first script around a part he'd created especially for the Manchester-born actress Violet Carson, who was already well-known for her work on stage and in the BBC's radio plays.

Tony was of the opinion that, while he was very pleased with his script, it was unlikely that it would have much appeal beyond the local area. Having read it, I was not much more optimistic. It was very good but its appeal seemed limited by its geographical setting. Would the rest of Britain be interested in a single street in the north? Tony and I went out in Manchester for the evening and I tried to be more encouraging about his idea. As we headed home, we passed a department store, and Tony told me that if Florizel Street was picked up nationwide, he would buy me anything I wanted from the shop window.

When Tony first submitted his script to Sidney Bernstein, Granada's founder, he received a swift rejection but producer Harry Elton saw the script's potential and commissioned an initial run of 13 episodes. The show opened with Violet Carson as Ena Sharples, widowed caretaker of the Glad Tidings Mission Hall, wearing her trademark hairnet. The street was renamed Coronation Street.

Of course the show became a huge success – when honouring Tony, the Royal Television Society declared Coronation Street to be 'the most successful show in television history' – and Tony did take me back to that Manchester department store to buy that reward for my support. I chose a set of serving dishes, which I kept for many years.

Unfortunately, the dishes were lost when the dresser where they lived suddenly tipped over, smashing every piece of crockery I'd ever collected. My Coronation Street dishes were unsalvageable but I still smile every time I hear that familiar theme tune and think of Tony bringing me that first script more than 60 years ago.

CHAPTER FORTY-THREE

Pat

In 1964, with a great deal of production experience under my belt, I left Granada and moved to the BBC. While still at Granada, I'd worked as producer on 'University Challenge' with Bamber Gascoigne in the quizmaster's chair. The show in that format, with Bamber at the helm, ran for 25 years and 913 episodes. In 1994, the format was revived by the BBC with Jeremy Paxman taking Bamber Gascoigne's place.

My brief when I arrived at the BBC in the mid-'60s was simple: I was to create studio-based entertainment – like University Challenge – on a much tighter budget. There was no money for fancy formats or celebrity guests. I'd have to rely on the general public wanting to take part. That is how 'Ask The Family' was born. The show consisted of a general knowledge quiz between two families of four. We had no shortage of families wanting to be on television and the show soon came together. The host was Robert Robinson, a journalist and film critic, who had previously presented 'Open House' and 'Take It Or Leave It'.

Doing things on a shoestring extended to recording some shows in my own home. By now I was married to Ray and we were living in Chiswick, in west London. I remember one summer using our house as the setting for a Christmas appeal.

In the '70s, BBC Television broadcast a five-minute appeal every month for a selected charity. Since such appeals were usually recorded well ahead of broadcast, on a blazing hot day in July, we put up a Christmas tree and hung tinsel from the lampshades. I roped in a group of friends to pretend they were attending a Christmas party.

Halfway through the filming, the doorbell rang. It was the milkman. I could tell that he was interested to see the Christmas decorations hanging in the hallway. I tried to explain that we were filming a Christmas show but he wouldn't let me finish.

'That's all right,' he told me. 'Lots of the people around here are on drugs. I just thought "there go Mr and Mrs Davies".'

It was the 1960s, I suppose.

One emergency appeal in particular lives on in my memory. It was in December 1972, following a devastating earthquake in Nicaragua.

My parents were elderly by this time and loved us all to be together at Newland Hall for Christmas. I had driven there with my husband Ray and my stepdaughter Ruth. Ray was at that time producing 'The World Tonight'.

News of the devastating earthquake broke just as we arrived in north Lancashire. I knew the BBC would want to film a special appeal to raise funds for those affected. Usually our appeals were organised months in advance but this was one we needed to react to quickly and I felt the full weight of responsibility.

I wanted someone who knew Nicaragua to make the appeal on camera. I was sure I must know someone but my address book was in my office at Kensington House. I rang the commissionaire on duty, who found the book and gave me the numbers I needed. I shall always be grateful to him for that. I spent Christmas Day making phone calls in my father's chilly gunroom, missing lunch with the family and working late into the night. It being Christmas, many people didn't pick up. However, Ray rang Jim Biddulph, TV News Diplomatic Correspondent, and found him at home. Jim was able to get hold of the British Ambassador to Nicaragua, Ivor Vincent, who was in England for the holidays. He in turn suggested that Dame Margot Fonteyn, the ballerina, might like to front the appeal. Thanks to the BBC ballet producer Margaret Dale, I tracked Dame Margot down. She agreed at once to take part.

At 4.30am on Boxing Day I jumped into the car with Ray and Ruth and a flask of black coffee and headed back to London, to start putting the broadcast together.

We began work later that morning. Denis Mann of the Secretariat cleared the appeal with Lord Hill and it was scheduled to be aired on the Wednesday. At 10.30 we met Denis at Television Centre. He had made over 40 calls from his home in Kingston to keep the necessary BBC departments informed.

Dame Margot arrived and worked on the script until lunchtime, missing her regular ballet practice. Meanwhile, News VT compiled shots from Nicaragua, the newsroom provided agency tapes, the BBC Library supplied information and emergency graphics were called in. At 8pm recording started in Presentation Studio A with John Longley directing.

By this time the Nicaraguan Ambassador in Britain, Signor Parrales, had also become involved. He brought brochures and pictures of the country. The taxi driver who drove him not only refused the fare but also gave him £1 towards the fund. This type of generosity was typical of the whole operation.

The weather broadcast was moved to Presentation B so recording could continue. By nine in the evening it was complete. The appeal also went out on radio the next day. Looking at my notes from that time I saw that within a few days I had written, 'So far over £160,000 has come in. It was a grand team effort'.

I made a range of appeals for various charities with many lovely people. John Le Mesurier of 'Dad's Army' was every bit as charming as his character Sgt Wilson, while Ronnie Corbett had me doubled over with laughter from the moment he walked onto the set.

I was very nervous about directing Richard Attenborough, such an eminent film director. I need not have worried. He was kindness itself.

As was customary, I booked a table for lunch at a restaurant ahead of filming so that we could make a plan. What remains in my mind is that, perhaps guessing that my budget would be very tight, Lord Attenborough was the only one of all the celebrities I worked with who insisted that he, and not the BBC, would pay for lunch.

By now I was quite senior at the BBC but there were still some people who were surprised to find themselves reporting to a female producer. Sexism was alive and well. I remember one young man, who had just joined my team, saying, 'After everything, I never thought I'd have to work for a woman.' I responded, 'Well, there you are,' and left him in no doubt that he'd just have to get on with it.

I worked at the BBC until my retirement in the late 1970s, after which I continued to work as a freelance producer for a while. My career in television spanned three very exciting decades but by far the highlight of my career was working on 'The Sky At Night'. I was a producer on the star-gazing show for eight years, during which time I was lucky enough to witness some of the most extraordinary astronomical events of the 20th century.

I travelled the world with presenter Sir Patrick Moore, famous for his idiosyncratic way of speaking and his monocle, who became a close friend. Together we covered the longest eclipse of the century from Mauritania. We also travelled to Russia, and, most thrilling of all, covered the 1969 moon landing from Houston, Texas.

The journey to Texas was an adventure in itself. At one point, we found ourselves sitting in an airport in the middle of nowhere, waiting for a plane to be repaired. The airline staff had told us that one of the engines was on the blink. I sat there in a quandary, wondering whether I ought to insist we waited for another flight. The BBC would never forgive me if the flight went down with one of their most valuable presenters on board.

I was in a panic but Patrick was completely relaxed. He wandered off and returned wearing an enormous Stetson. The sheer sight of him in a monocle and a ten-gallon-hat was enough to put me at ease. The engine was fixed, we boarded the flight and all was well.

I met astronaut Neil Armstrong, the first man to walk on the moon, when he came to the United Kingdom for interviews a few months after his historic mission. When his team struggled to find him a suitable hotel in the north of England, I suggested that he stay at Newland Hall. My parents were delighted at the idea. Armstrong took me up on the offer and a few days later he was safely installed in Lancashire, taking tea with my mother and playing billiards with my father. Jean was at Newland at the time and remembers walking into the room and thinking: 'How extraordinary to think that the man playing billiards with Daddy has walked on the moon.'

Newland Hall had seen it all, from gavottes to astronauts. What a wonderful privilege it was to be able to bring such an extraordinary man to our family home.

CHAPTER FORTY-FOUR

Jean

I had had a very interesting and exciting time since the end of the war, but as I reached my late-'30s, I paused to look back over my life and my career, and realised that since I turned 18 and joined the FANY, I'd held 17 jobs in seven countries. I'd worked in code and cipher, in refugee work and social work. I'd had secretarial stints for UNESCO, for the government in Malawi, and at Oxford University. Mine was the curriculum vitae of a woman who couldn't settle down. Suddenly, with my 40th birthday looming on the horizon, it felt like the time to try.

In the summer of 1964, I was working for a charity campaign in London when I heard that a new university was being built in Lancaster. After a few years in the capital, the thought of going back to the county of my childhood was very appealing, so I wrote a letter, asking if there was any interesting work going. I received only a rejection. I thought that was that, but a few days later, I received a telephone call from the new university's Vice-Chancellor, Charles Carter, offering me a job as a fundraiser. Just as when Fitzroy Maclean invited me to join him at the Refugee Commission, I jumped at the chance. The fundraising campaign went well, and a year later, Charles offered me a new challenge.

He wanted to know whether I would be interested in setting up a department offering careers advice. Such a thing was a relatively new concept for a British university.

But career advice? Me? The idea of setting up a whole department was certainly interesting but how could I possibly advise university students on their post-graduation options when I didn't even have a degree myself? Charles Carter didn't think that was a problem. He was of the view that my unusual background, having worked in so many different jobs in so many different places, would be an asset. I may not have a degree but I had real life experience by the bucket-load. I told him I would take the job.

I felt very lucky to have Charles Carter behind me. From the beginning, he encouraged me to 'look after the ones who are failing. Don't worry too much about the successes'. That appealed to the old social worker in me. I threw myself into the role and didn't look back.

Though I had no real template, I didn't entirely make it up as I went along. I spent some time shadowing careers officers at other universities. I travelled to the United States and saw how they were doing things there. Then I tore up the rule book.

My approach to careers advice was somewhat based on my approach to personal relationships. I always insisted on having a full hour for a first meeting with any student who wanted to use the service. If you're meeting a stranger, you need to establish a relationship before you can truly begin to help them. You need to find out what makes them tick. You have to have a sense of a person before you can understand their ambitions and their needs. It wasn't enough to know what someone was studying and where they 'ought' to be headed with their qualifications. I wanted to know 'who is this person at heart?' A personal relationship was crucial. At the same time, I always used to say to my students that ultimately, if you want something, it is up to you to go and find it – to use your initiative. You know you better than I do, so only you know what you are capable of. I looked upon my role as giving people the tools and the confidence to find their own way.

As the careers department became busier, I very much enjoyed helping people to work out what they really wanted to do. As Charles Carter had predicted, it was the ones who had no clue how to go about finding work who interested me most.

There was one student, whom I called 'our revolutionary leader!' He led all the campus protests and got involved in all the causes, but he had no idea what he wanted to do. He did try applying to one or two companies who had jobs going, but he never got beyond an interview. I was so pleased when one day he shouted out to me, as we passed in the street, 'I got one!' – a job that is – and it was because he had finally taken my friendly advice to try wearing a jacket. He was a maverick, but I liked him because he was interested and he *listened* because, I think, he liked me too. That was the importance of creating a relationship in action.

I have visited Lancaster University many times since I retired. It was a joy to be invited to talk to the current careers team a few years ago. They are able to offer the students much more than we could back in the 1960s, though I think the same spirit prevails. LU was always a very friendly and warm place, totally different from the stuffy older establishments. There was always a sense that everyone working and studying there wanted to make the experience of higher education a truly enriching one, accessible by all.

One thing that pleases me enormously is how many women attend university these days. As Pat already mentioned, as children, she and I were told that we should not expect to go to university. Our family did not have enough money to educate all three of us to degree level and, as son and heir, our brother Bob was the priority. Though I never studied for a degree, I do think that being told that higher education was a male privilege made me all the more determined to prove that women can do anything they set their minds to.

Joining the FANY helped me to break free of the restrictions of my age and class. By the time I came back from Bari at the end of the war, I knew that I could never settle down to the life that might have been expected of me and I didn't. I always told my female students, 'You have to get over the 'only a woman' attitude.' The number of female students attending university today prove that it works.

When I joined the team at Lancaster University, not only had I at last found a career I could settle down to, I found myself a husband too. At 40 years old, I had rather given up on the idea of ever getting married. My husband Mike Argles was the new university's librarian. We fell in love. I became step-mother to his lovely children and we settled in the cottage in Wray.

After we both retired in 1980, Mike and I were lucky enough to have time to travel to all the places I had previously travelled to alone and many more besides. Alas, we didn't have many years together. I was widowed in my fifties. But we had a very happy marriage and for that I thank my lucky stars that I took that careers service job at LU.

My advice to any young person today would be to travel if they are able, and make sure to meet people from different backgrounds. Try new places and have a go at things. That was the advice our father always gave us. There's nothing to be lost by trying. Always say 'yes' to the opportunities that come your way, even if you think – as at first I did when I was offered that careers role at Lancaster – that you're not ready. There's no room for imposter syndrome in an exciting life!

At the same time, if you find yourself in a situation that doesn't suit you – for example, you are in a job that makes you unhappy, even if it is high-status and well-paid – don't be afraid to cut your losses and move on. During my time in the careers service, I often came across young people who were following a particular career path because they felt they ought to, who worried that if they admitted that they weren't enjoying the vocation they had chosen and gave up on it, they would be deemed to have failed. Ignore talk about failure. There is no such thing. Tell yourself you're not failing, only deciding not to waste your time and looking for a situation that suits you better. Nobody benefits from your being unhappy, least of all you. This is the view I have always taken. It didn't always go down well with my employers (particularly when I was on secondment to a careers service at a certain university in the United States), but I firmly believe that happiness is more important than any amount of money or prestige. Personally, I always rather liked it when things went wrong, offering up the opportunity for an unexpected adventure.

I would also advise anyone – at least from time to time – to listen to their older sister. I treat Pat's opinions with the greatest respect. I have made my own way through life but it's always been better when I've sought Pat's help. It's wonderful to have a companion through the years.

It's also been wonderful to have the chance to share my experiences in this book and in 'Codebreaking Sisters'. The round of book fairs and history festivals we've enjoyed these past few years are so unlike my normal quiet country life it has come as rather a surprise in my nineties! However, I am getting quite used to it and shall be sorry when it all dies down. I'm still ready for the next adventure.

CHAPTER FORTY-FIVE

Pat

On September 8th 1939, less than a week after the declaration of war, our father turned 40. I was 16 years old at the time and found the idea of being so very ancient – 40 that is – quite distasteful. I wrote in my diary, 'Daddy's 40th birthday! May I die before I'm 40! Why should we grow old – shrewish middle age; shaking, half-dead old age – why spoil all joyful memory of life – of proper life, full-blooded youth, by the anticlimactic ending of slow decay?'

How I'd like to take that passionate young girl by the hand and tell her that getting older really isn't that bad. 40, in particular, seems terribly young to me now. Our father, just entering 'shrewish middle age' had so much ahead of him, not least his three years as a prisoner of war.

Returning from the Far East, our father Cary, our handsome, funny Daddy, went back to work at Cliff Mill. In later life, he became the High Sheriff of Lancashire and was given an OBE for his services to the textile industry. He had a very happy retirement, but his one regret was that he had been unable to find a publisher for his POW diaries. Throughout his internment, our father had kept a diary, hiding the notebooks into which he scribbled the daily record inside hollow bamboo poles. As each book was filled, our father would bury them in a grave in the camp's cemetery, where they remained until he and his men were liberated.

I knew how important it was to our father to see his writing gain a wider audience, not just for his own satisfaction but to pass on the stories of the men with whom he had shared those difficult times. And not only for his fellow soldiers, but also for the local people who had helped them at great risk to their own safety.

In 1964, while I was still at Granada, I travelled to Thailand to cover a United Nations conference. Thailand had always loomed large in my imagination as the place where our father spent three years as a prisoner. It was with some trepidation that I decided that while I was in the country, I would try to visit Chungkai, where he had been held.

In his diary, our father had written about a local man, a Bangkok merchant called Ah Boon Pong, who put his own life in danger to save thousands of British prisoners by smuggling food and drugs into the Japanese prison camps. After the war, he was decorated for his valiant service.

It seemed to me that Boon Pong was the person I most needed to meet if I was to find out more about those awful years. Luckily, Boon Pong was easily found and agreed to meet me. He drove me to see the sites of the former camps, which was a desperately moving experience. Then Boon Pong took me to his home, where he showed me a chair.

'In that,' he told me. 'Your father sat to have lunch the day after the war ended.'

The thought of Daddy, free at last, sharing a meal with

his friend, made me very happy indeed. But though several local newspapers – and the Granada in-house magazine – reported on my pilgrimage to meet Boon Pong, it seemed that no one wanted to hear the full story of my father's time in Thailand. Those notebooks, which might have cost him his life had the Japanese found them in their hiding place, languished in the study at Newland Hall.

After our father died in 1993, my brother Bob returned to England to clear Newland Hall ready for sale. By this time, Bob was settled in South Africa and had no intention of coming back to Lancashire. Bob took our father's POW diaries with him to South Africa, where they remained unread since tragically, not long afterwards, Bob was cruelly murdered by an intruder at his home.

Years later, Bob's widow asked me if I would like to have a copy of Daddy's diaries. I jumped at the chance, and was surprised and moved all over again by my father's account of those years in Chungkai. I shared them with Jean. Knowing how much it had meant to our father that his experiences and those of his fellow prisoners be remembered, we had the diaries typed up and decided to have one last shot at getting them published.

Since our father's attempts to get the diaries published had met with such indifference, we didn't really expect much luck, but not long after we sent the manuscript out, we received a letter from Pen And Sword Books, saying that they would very much like to take the project on. The diaries became a book called '1,000 Days on the River Kwai'. The original notebooks are now in the care of the Imperial War Museum.

Our father's book opened up a whole new world for Jean and me, as we embarked upon a book tour, speaking about both our father's wartime experiences and our own. We were surprised and delighted to find that people seemed interested in our careers in the women's services and very much enjoyed talking about those years at schools, history festivals and book clubs. All the same, we were astonished when our friend Simon Robinson suggested we write a memoir of our own.

We are the only living sisters to have signed the Official Secrets Act in World War Two. We took the provisions of the Act so seriously that it wasn't until we were well into middle age that we dared to ask each other what we had done during the war. We certainly never expected that one day we would be sharing our secrets in a book!

Jean and I published our own first volume of memoirs, 'Codebreaking Sisters: Our Secret War', at the height of the Covid pandemic, which rather put paid to our plans for another book tour. Stuck at different ends of the country, we wrote to each other many times a week and telephoned every day. Lockdown was no fun at all – who would have thought life could suddenly be so very dreary – but it provided us with an opportunity to sit quietly and reflect and write down some of the memories which are included here. All the same, we were very glad when we were able to start socialising on a relatively normal basis again and were able to celebrate in the garden when we heard that 'Codebreaking Sisters' had reached *The Sunday Times* bestsellers list. As Jean put it, it's all rather different from the quiet old age we expected but what fun it has been!

And now I'm just a few months away from my hundredth birthday. I can't quite believe it. I'm mostly surprised to have reached an age that no-one in our family has ever reached before. The 1920s don't seem terribly long ago. I still feel as though I'm waiting for it all to start.

These days, neither one of us is able to drive and, since the Covid pandemic, travelling by train is not the appealing option it once was. Fortunately, we are lucky to have family members and friends willing to make the drive between London and Lancaster, with one or other of us in the back, so that we can still spend time with each other regularly.

In November 2022, together with our friend Simon Robinson, we were able to be together in Lancaster for the opening of a new exhibition at the city museum which featured a tableau dedicated to our war years. The following day, we made a pilgrimage of sorts to Dolphinholme, the village of our childhood, where we attended a service of remembrance at St Mark's Church and afterwards laid a wreath in memory of the fallen. It was a task which our father usually carried out, no doubt thinking as he did so of the friends and colleagues he lost in Singapore and Chungkai.

It was a deeply-affecting moment for both of us. As we sat in our old family pew and talked to the vicar, we couldn't help but reflect on those Sunday mornings long past, when we sat alongside our parents, our grandfather and our little brother Bob – always turning round to gaze at Dora Gort on the pew behind. Outside in the church yard, we visited the graves of Grandboffin and Effie, of our beloved parents, and of our kind Uncle Tom and our glamorous Aunt Gioia. We paid our respects to Lilly – Cecelie Getzl – whose gentle influence changed our lives forever, setting us off on such adventures. Her headstone was crowned by a beautiful red rose bush. Then we stood side by side by the stone cross carved with our family name to look out over the soft grey-green fells, so unchanged since we were children.

By the time this book is published, we will have shared more than 98 years of sisterhood. Though at times, we have led very different lives and lived many miles apart, we have always remained close. Not a week has gone by when we haven't been in touch by letter, telegram or telephone. There is something very special about having someone by your side who has known you for practically your whole life. When we are together, we still have a great deal of fun. We are each others' nearest and dearest.

How lucky we are to have lived through one of the most exciting periods in history. How lucky we are to have had so many adventures. And how lucky we are to have had one another through the years.

At the beginning of March 2023, Jean travelled to London with our friend Simon Robinson so that we could read through the manuscript which would become the book you now hold in your hand. On the journey from Lancashire, they stopped at a service station and as they ate a sandwich and watched the comings and goings, Jean recited for Simon one of her favourite poems, 'Leisure' by the Welsh poet W.H. Davies, which famously begins: 'What is this life if, full of care, we have no time to stand and stare?' She later told Simon, 'One doesn't expect to live to be almost 100, but it has been an interesting life and I must say I have enjoyed it.'

When Jean and Simon arrived at my house in Chiswick, we had a whiskey and soda and listened to old recordings of sentimental songs from the 1940s. Jean sang 'Lili Marlene' in Italian. I sang the same song in German. Then Simon joined in with the English version. At the weekend, we went to the Cadogan Hall together to watch The Chelsea Opera Group sing Tchaikovsky's 'Oprichnik'. Jean very much enjoyed the music and the interval ice-cream. Many of our friends were in the chorus and in the audience alongside us.

A few days later, Jean was very unwell. We called a doctor

and she was taken into Charing Cross Hospital. I was hopeful that it would be for just a few days. I visited Jean daily, supported by our cousin Sarah, Maribel and Dinah and various other friends. But despite our best hopes, Jean was moved from the hospital to a hospice in Ealing. I continued to spend as much time with her there as I could.

My cousin Sarah, who was a palliative care nursing sister, has been an immeasurable support during Jean's illness and beyond. In Jean's room at the hospice, while my sister slept, we talked of this being Jean's final journey. We spoke about our last trip to the opera together and agreed that however hard it was, it was a privilege to be with her at the end. Judy, Jean's step daughter, talked with Jean about seeing her late husband Mike again and their dogs. I reminisced about the many adventures Jean and I had together, our travels and even our childhood 'pretends'.

Recently, I found a letter I wrote to our mother in June 1946, thanking her for my birthday gifts, in which I recounted a June spent with Jean (at that time known as Jinks), while I was working for the Embassy in Norway. Jean and I had a cocktail party at my flat to celebrate my turning 23. While I had embassy duties, Jean went for swims in the fjord and attended midsummer bonfires with naval cadets and other friends of ours. I finished the letter by describing a trip we were to make across Scandinavia. My closing line was, 'What fun to be able to spend my financial presents on foreign travel! Nothing could be better or more exciting, especially with dear Jinks.'

It was true. Nothing was better than travels with my sister.

How lucky I am to have had her for so long and have travelled so widely with her.

In the days leading to Jean's final moments the blossom gathered on the trees outside her window, promising the arrival of spring. I thought of how summer had always suited Jean best and the words 'Fear no more the heat of the sun' from Shakespeare's *Cymbeline* came into my head. Summer was Jean's favourite season.

While Sarah and I sat with Jean in the early hours of the morning of April 2nd, a brave robin sang his heart out in the darkness. There followed a premature dawn chorus that offered comfort. A short while later, Jean passed away.

How empty the world has suddenly become. Jean was always the first person I would talk to. I was always her older sister and now she has gone after 97 years with me. I don't know why I should have outlived her. I wanted Jean to be with me at my 100th birthday party but now I will use it to remember and celebrate her as I will do for the remainder of my life. I miss her but I would not have wanted her to suffer. I will carry her memory with me always.

Patricia Davies

Acknowledgements

On behalf of Jean and myself, I would especially like to thank Chris Manby for all her hard work in preparing this book and for her friendship. I am also very grateful to my friend and agent Simon Robinson for his support and for helping make this part of our lives more interesting. Thanks also to Steve Hanrahan, Paul Dove, Christine Costello and the rest of the team at Mirror Books.

Thanks are due to Jordan, Sian, Tizzy and Gintare, who supported Jean at home in Lancashire. Also to Sue and Neil, Jean's friends and neighbours from the marvellous George & Dragon in Wray, with whom we enjoyed many excellent meals.

A special thank you to Maribel Seno and Edwina "Dinah" Veras who devotedly sat in the hospital each day supporting Jean and me during her illness. I would also like to thank all of the doctors and nurses at Charing Cross Hospital and Meadow House Hospice for their care. There are in addition a lot of friends in Chiswick and elsewhere that I would like to acknowledge and thank and they will know who they are.

I would particularly like to mention my cousin Sarah Folland, who sat alongside me every day during Jean's last weeks. Likewise, I know Jean would want me to thank her stepchildren Judy, Gill and Antony Argles, and her five step-grandchildren and seven step-great-grandchildren for their care, love and devotion and endless support.

9ᵗʰ June 1929. A picnic at Red on Marsham. Jill her Nannie, Jean, Pat, Aunty Doll, Pat Watt Cary, Paul & Christopher.

Mrs Kok & me in my nursery. I am one day old. That is my cot behind me; it is covered in a little pink frills, & it has bunches of roses & forget me nots here & there.

Grannie & me. I am three days old.

Tuesday 13ᵗʰ Aug. Mrs Kok & my bear. Cousin Gerry gave it to me when she came to tea.

Friday 1ˢᵗ Aug Grandpapa & Grandma & me. Monday & Nanny & I motored to Preston in Irish?

Grandpapa, Grannie & me

Volume V

30 Days — JUNE
— Summer Solstice · Longest Day
...
7 Feb. 1929. When Windermere froze Uncle Sidney, Jean, Pat ...

APRIL

3 Sat

o-asks tv producer Pat
...at kind of a Christmas
...eds plenty of time to
...wer.
Christmas Day making at
...hone calls and at 4:45 on

flask of black coffee in Television Centre.
She was en route to produce an
emergency appeal for the Nicaraguan
earthquake.
Dozens of BBC staff, were involved in
complex arrangements to get the appeal
on BBC 1 at 10.45 pm on 27 December.

Denis Mann of Secretariat rang Pat in
Lancaster where she had gone for
Christmas with her husband Ray Davies
of *The World Tonight* and her daughter
Ruth, a secretary at Registry. He told her
that a request for an appeal had been
cleared by Lord Hill and it was likely to
...be scheduled by Paul Fox for Wednesday

Recalling N-W space explore

...first to discover the Transit
...Venus.

...this was the first venture
...into "space" geometry. By
...watching its dark star of
...the event the face of the
...using incandescent polish
...had the earth, internal
...calculating were able to
...sure the distance of the
...from the sun.
...it was 11.05 that the

STRICTLY PRIVATE

Mrs. ...ham,
St... H...

Three days old Grandname in the ...

...m. All clear just gone ...
..., during which I had a ...
... of the window, + π put ...
...acks, got the warning (red) +
...2 alarms which Daddy was ...
...they
...each
...ms to ...
...ale no ...
...Buck ...
...spitals + ...
...nest St. ...
...ffice, of ...
...b. Phil ...
...the D.S.C
...action
...for which h...

...ppeal

(from page 1)

Margaret Dale, Pat tracked Dame Mar...
to a London hotel and left a message...
'The rest of the family were...
Christmas lunch,' said Pat. 'I sat in...
father's unheated gunroom where...
keeps the phone,' Dame Margar...
from London that night and agreed...
the appeal.
On Boxing morning Pat, her hu...
and daughter who also offered to...
were up at 4 am to drive to Lon...
10.30 they met Denis Mann at...
had made over 40 calls from his...
Kingston to keep the necessar...
departments informed. Dame...
worked on the script until hu...
missing her regular ballet practice...
News VT compiled shot...
Nicaragua - Newsroom provide...
tapes, Library supplied inf...
emergency graphics were c...
presentation staff on duty...
Hubbard, Nick Franks, John F...
and Bruce Goddard — were

Pat *Wean* + *their* aununts
Probably taken in the *spring* of
Pat's *beloved* Koko is *sitting*
...days head.

Special Examination for HC
of M.A.

13

Candidate's Name.

Ethel Pat

SO BRIEFLY OURS

There blows a winter leaf along the grass
And now must come to pass
The sad, unwilling miracle again:
Another Autumn blown with withered haste
Along the waste
Inexorable infinity of time,
O soundless chime
That tolls the dooms of pleasure and of pain,
Though to yourself such clemency be treason,
Still, still your knell, have pity and refrain!
Spare us this Season!
Let it one day, one hour too long remain.

Though you old skinflint Time must bear away
Your harvest of a day
To swell the gold heaped in your granaries,
Miserly grudging us the lovely hours
So briefly ours,
Yet your all-reaping blade cannot remove
That which our love
Has in your spite made timeless. Look, in this
We have cheated you! Fool, get you behind us.

Yet in the very moment of our bliss
He will remind us
That worms at last shall crawl where now we kiss.

Patricia Owtram, 1950